"*Mystagogy of the Eucharist* is an excellen
practice and theory. The reflective proc
ministers and teachers enables both the
more fully understand the biblical proc
one's life."

> —Catherine Dooley, OP, emerita,
> Catholic University of America
> Washington, DC

"Anyone who has been involved in the study and practice of liturgical
catechesis over the past twenty five years has benefitted from the work of
Gilbert Ostdiek. *Mystagogy of the Eucharist* offers a brilliant synthesis: an
engaging framework for mystagogical reflection and its flexible application to
each segment of the eucharistic liturgy. What do we do? What does it mean?
Whether you are reading this as a liturgist, catechist, or first time participant
in mystagogical reflection upon the experience of Eucharist, you cannot
help but be drawn into mystery. In responding to the church's call for new
evangelization, I highly recommend this text for anyone facilitating parish
faith development or religious formation."

> —Mary Ann Clarahan, RSM
> Professor of Liturgy and Sacraments
> Pontificio Collegio Beda, Rome

"Many people have come to associate mystagogy with the rites of Initiation,
it being in the narrow sense the period between Easter and Pentecost.
But mystagogy is more than a period of time; it is a way of knowing from
ritual experience. Gil Ostdiek applies this principle as he reflects upon the
Eucharist drawing upon the liturgical symbols, prayer texts, and ritual
actions of the Mass. He provides a wonderful pastoral resource for liturgical
ministers and those responsible for liturgical formation. Anyone reading this
book will come to savor the liturgy to a greater extent knowing the Eucharist
from within."

> —Michael S. Driscoll, Professor of Liturgical Studies
> and Sacred Music at the University of Notre Dame

"The paschal mystery is the key to understanding our lives as Christians. In
Fr. Gilbert Ostdiek's *Mystagogy of the Eucharist,* pastors and catechists have an
invaluable resource to deepen their community's celebration, understanding,
and participation in the Eucharist, which is our communal and individual
entry into the paschal mystery."

> —Rev. Joseph E. Weiss, SJ, Pastor
> Saint Thomas More Catholic Community
> Saint Paul, Minnesota

Mystagogy of the Eucharist
A Resource for Faith Formation

Gilbert Ostdiek, OFM

LITURGICAL PRESS
Collegeville, Minnesota

www.litpress.org

The Scripture quotations contained herein are from the New Revised Standard Version, copyright © 1989 by the Division of Christian Education of the National Council of the Churches of Christ in the U.S.A., and are used by permission. All rights reserved.

Excerpts reprinted from the English translation of *The Roman Missal* © 2010, International Commission on English in the Liturgy Corporation. All rights reserved.

Excerpts reprinted from *Guide for the Assembly* by Cardinal Joseph Bernardin © 1997, Archdiocese of Chicago: Liturgy Training Publications, www.LTP.org. All rights reserved. Used with permission.

Excerpts reprinted from *Guide for Sunday Mass* by Cardinal Roger Mahony © 1997, Archdiocese of Chicago: Liturgy Training Publications, www.LTP.org. All rights reserved. Used with permission.

Excerpts from "The Great Tablecloth" from *Extravagaria* by Pablo Neruda, translated by Alastair Reid. Translation copyright © 1974 by Alastair Reid. Reprinted by permission of Farrar, Straus and Giroux, LLC.

Poetry from *Liturgical Gestures Words Objects* edited by Eleanor Bernstein, CSJ © 1995, Notre Dame Center for Pastoral Liturgy. All rights reserved. Used with permission.

1   2   3   4   5   6   7   8   9

Library of Congress Cataloging-in-Publication Data

Ostdiek, Gilbert.
  Mystagogy of the Eucharist : a resource for Faith Formation / Gilbert Ostdiek, OFM.
    pages   cm
    ISBN 978-0-8146-3719-7 — ISBN 978-0-8146-3744-9 (ebook)
  1. Lord's Supper—Catholic Church.   2. Lord's Supper (Liturgy)   I. Title.
BX2215.3.O88   2015
264'.02036—dc23   2014042572

Contents

Preface

This little book is the product of many people. The contents have been field tested over a number of years with many participants in workshops and sessions of mystagogical reflection on the Eucharist, including parishioners, clergy, and graduate theology students. To them I owe grateful thanks for their responses and suggestions. I also wish to thank my faculty colleagues at Catholic Theological Union who have been a constant source of inspiration and support in so many ways. I especially owe a debt of gratitude to all the staff at Liturgical Press, who have been most solicitous, patient, and helpful in bringing this volume to publication. Finally, I wish to express my deepest thanks to my family and friends, my Franciscan confreres and students, all of whom have taught me so much about how liturgy speaks to us and what it means for our lives. Above all, to our gracious and loving God, be all thanks, honor, and glory.

Gilbert Ostdiek, OFM
Professor of Liturgy
Catholic Theological Union

Abbreviations

RB   *The Rule of St. Benedict* (Collegeville, MN: Liturgical Press, 1981).

CCC   *Catechism of the Catholic Church* (John Paul II, 1992)

DOL   *Documents on the Liturgy* (Collegeville, MN: Liturgical Press, 1982)

GDC   *General Directory for Catechesis* (Congregation for the Clergy, 1997)

GILM   *General Introduction to the Lectionary for Mass* (Congregation for Divine Worship and the Discipline of the Sacraments, ICEL translation, 1998)

GIRM   *General Instruction of the Roman Missal* (ICEL translation, 2010)

LG   *Lumen Gentium*: Dogmatic Constitution on the Church (Vatican II, November 21, 1964)

LGWO   *Liturgical Gestures Words Objects*, ed. Eleanor Bernstein (Notre Dame Center for Pastoral Liturgy, 1995)

MR   *Missale Romanum*: The Roman Missal, 3rd edition (ICEL Translation, 2010)

OM   The Order of Mass, in *Missale Romanum*, 3rd edition (ICEL Translation, 2010)

SC   *Sacrosanctum Concilium*: The Constitution on the Sacred Liturgy (Vatican II, December 4, 1963)

Introduction

Why this book?

Why did they change the Mass? Does that change what the Mass itself means? These questions were often asked when the revised *Roman Missal* was implemented in Roman Catholic communities at the beginning of Advent 2011. To be sure, there were many well-designed programs of preparation. Much of the material for that preparation focused, however, on what changes were being made in the new translations and why,[1] or on the theology of the revised texts.[2] Others gave the historical and theological background for each part of the revised Mass.[3] Questions people asked gave voice to a thirst for something beyond instructions or academic theology. People still feel a persistent hunger to know what the Eucharist means for their daily living, to connect liturgy and life. That is the hunger this book seeks to address.

To explore what the Eucharist can mean for daily living, *Mystagogy of the Eucharist: A Resource for Faith Formation*, takes an approach that differs from many of the available resources. It offers a mystagogy of the Eucharist, that is, a reflective walk-through. It asks two simple questions about the Eucharist: What do we do? And what does that mean? Toward that end, the book takes the ritual actions of the Eucharist as its starting

---

[1] E.g., Paul Turner, *Understanding the Revised Mass Texts*, 2nd ed. (Chicago: Liturgy Training Publications, 2010).

[2] Barry Hudock, *The Eucharistic Prayer: A User's Guide* (Collegeville, MN: Liturgical Press, 2010), focuses specifically on the Eucharistic Prayer. For a publication focused on the homiletic and catechetical potential of the revised texts, see Anscar J. Chupungco, *The Prayers of the New Missal: A Homiletic and Catechetical Companion* (Collegeville, MN: Liturgical Press, 2013).

[3] E.g., Paul Turner, *At the Supper of the Lamb: A Pastoral and Theological Commentary on the Mass* (Chicago: Liturgy Training Publications, 2011).

point. It then draws on liturgical symbols, prayer texts, and reflective commentary to explore what meaning those ritual actions can have for Christian living.

This book is offered primarily as a pastoral resource for those who are responsible for the formation of worshippers and their liturgical ministers. Chief among those who bear this responsibility are directors of liturgy, those who prepare liturgical ministers, RCIA directors and catechists, and especially directors of religious education and of adult faith formation. It might also be of use in campus ministry and retreat settings. Though this book has been written from a Roman Catholic context and perspective, others are also invited to borrow freely and adapt whatever may be of use in their own contexts. The ultimate goal is that *Mystagogy of the Eucharist* will help all who participate in the celebration of the Eucharist to name and reflect on the deeper meaning it has for daily living.

The plan of the book is simple. The first chapter in Part I will sketch some reminders about liturgy and mystagogy. Chapter 2 will offer a biblical model of mystagogy and describe some practical procedures and resources that can be used for it. Subsequent chapters in Part II will reflect on individual segments of the eucharistic rite: gathering, proclaiming and listening to the Word, presenting the gifts of bread and wine, offering thanks and oneself, breaking and sharing bread, being sent, and saying Amen.

Part I

Frameworks

1

Some Reminders

About liturgy

What is liturgy about? The Constitution on the Sacred Liturgy issued by Vatican II is very clear about it.[1] The paschal mystery lies at the heart of the liturgy. Christ "achieved his task of redeeming humanity and giving perfect glory to God, principally by the paschal mystery of his blessed passion, resurrection from the dead, and glorious ascension" (SC 5). The Constitution goes on to say: "In the liturgy by means of signs perceptible to the senses, human sanctification is signified and brought about in ways proper to each of these signs; in the liturgy the whole public worship is performed by the Mystical Body of Jesus Christ, that is, by the Head and his members" (SC 7).

Let's focus for a moment on the phrase "signs perceptible to the senses." What are those signs? The *Catechism of the Catholic Church* explains it this way.

> A sacramental celebration is woven from signs and symbols. In keeping with the divine pedagogy of salvation, their meaning is rooted in the work of creation and in human culture, specified by the events of the Old Covenant and fully revealed in the person and work of Christ. (CCC 1145)

[1] Vatican Council II, Constitution on the Sacred Liturgy (*Sacrosanctum Concilium*), ICEL translation, in *Documents on the Liturgy 1963–1979: Conciliar, Papal, and Curial Texts*, nos. 1–131 (Collegeville, MN: Liturgical Press, 1982). Translations of the Constitution are taken from this source and cited in text hereafter as SC. Also online at www.vatican.va/archive/hist_councils/ii_vatican_council/documents/vat-ii_const_19631204_sacrosanctum-concilium_en.html.

. . .

> The liturgical celebration involves signs and symbols relating to
> creation (candles, water, fire), human life (washing, anointing,
> breaking bread) and the history of salvation (the rites of the
> Passover). Integrated into the world of faith and taken up by
> the power of the Holy Spirit, these cosmic elements, human
> rituals, and gestures of remembrance of God become bearers of
> the saving and sanctifying action of Christ. (CCC 1189)

Liturgical signs and symbols, then, are built up of many layers:

- created realities that were meant to tell us something of their
  Creator;
- human and religious rituals that make use of these perceptible
  realities in social gestures that enable people to communicate with
  one another and with their gods;
- rituals of Jewish life that take up those human and religious rituals
  and transform them into gestures of remembrance of the covenant;
  and
- rituals from the life of Jesus and his early followers that further
  transform those Jewish rituals into gestures of remembrance of the
  covenant Jesus announced in word and deed and sealed with his
  death and resurrection.[2]

These liturgical signs and symbols make use of material realities, human
actions, and words. As the Constitution indicates, "human sanctification
is signified and brought about in ways proper to each of these signs" (SC
7). Classical theology spoke of the sacraments as working in both those
ways, i.e., signifying and effecting salvation. The stress, however, fell
more on their efficacy than on their communicative function. Current
theology has recovered and highlights the communicative function. The
sacramental signs themselves, prior to any theological reflection, say
what they do and do what they say. They are like God's creative word
(*dabar* in Hebrew): "God said 'let there be light'; and there was light"
(Gen 1:3). In the biblical way of thinking, words do things and deeds
speak. The Constitution encourages us to attend to that power of the
sacramental signs and symbols to say wordlessly what they bring about.

[2] Summarized from CCC 1146–52.

How do symbols communicate?[3] From its Greek roots the word "symbol" (*sym* + *ballein*) means to bring together what was apart. By mutually engaging our bodies and all our senses, human symbols make communication possible between people. Symbols are not just objects; they are symbols because of our actions, what we do with them. Think of actions like exchanging and wearing wedding rings or displaying and saluting flags. They not only engage the body, they speak to the heart without the need of words. They give expression to what is within us and communicate that to others through sound, sight, smile, touch, gesture. And when others receive this communication through their bodily senses, the magic happens. Our inner selves are in touch with each other, to share something of our dreams, our loves, our lives, our very selves.

Liturgical symbols work in that same way. They bring together our embodied selves and the hidden God we worship, who is present to us under tangible signs and symbols. Liturgy begins with our bodies. Think of baptismal washing with water, of sharing food and drink, of anointing someone with oil, and so on. Liturgical symbols begin with bodily action, but they do not end there; they lead to the mystery hidden within. Spiritual cleansing, nourishment of soul, healing of spirit. And marvel of marvels, the words of our liturgy tell us again and again that it is not just we who perform these holy human actions; rather, our liturgical action embodies that of Christ: "The Gospel of the Lord." "May the peace of Christ. . . ." Liturgical symbols are born for communication. They bespeak and bring to fruition all that unites us, especially the love of Christ and our love for one another. "People in love make signs of love."[4]

Liturgical catechesis, then, needs to attend to what the ritual actions of the liturgy have to say, not just in words, but by their very performance. According to the *Catechism*, that embodied meaning builds on the use of created things in human and Jewish rituals, and it transforms what those rituals say and do. That layering and transformation of meaning in liturgical rites will be of great importance for mystagogy, for it is in the liturgical rituals themselves that mystagogy begins.

---

[3] Some of the material in subsequent paragraphs is adapted from an earlier article, Gilbert Ostdiek, "Ongoing Mystagogy Begins in the Liturgy," *Pastoral Music* 25, no. 6 (Aug/Sept 2001): 21–22.

[4] Bishops Committee on the Liturgy, *Music in Catholic Worship* 4 (Washington, DC: National Conference of Catholic Bishops, 1972, revised ed.1983).

About mystagogy

When they hear the word "mystagogy," most people now connect it with the period in the catechumenate that follows the sacraments of initiation. To appreciate fully what mystagogy is and understand its role, we need to step back and place it in a larger framework. The church sees catechesis, that includes mystagogy, as a form of ministry of the Word. That ministry, in turn, is a "fundamental element" in what the church calls evangelization.[5] Another name for evangelization is the mission of the church. That mission is what Jesus entrusted to his disciples before his Ascension. "Go therefore and make disciples of all nations" (Matt 28:19). Their mission is to be an extension of his own. "As the Father has sent me, so I send you" (John 20:21). The church's mission is what God entrusted to Jesus. His shorthand name for his mission is the "reign of God." He was sent to announce it and bring it about. In that reign, attitudes and values of love, forgiveness, reconciliation, and invitation to all to sit at the table were foremost. For after all, the God who sent him "is love" (1 John 4:8).

The church's mission to bring about God's reign unfolds in four steps, church documents tell us (e.g., GDC 47–69). The first step is called *silent proclamation*. That is the living witness of Christ's disciples who by their lives show others what life in God's reign is to be like.[6] Silent witness is absolutely critical for the evangelization work to follow. Without it the following steps would not have credibility or succeed.

The second step is *missionary activity*, that is, the *explicit proclamation* of the gospel. We normally associate this with "missionaries," but we all have a part to play.[7] At the conclusion of every celebration of the Eucharist, we are all sent forth on mission, to proclaim the gospel and glorify God by how we live.

---

[5] Congregation for the Clergy, *General Directory for Catechesis*, 50 (Washington, DC: United States Catholic Conference, 1998). Hereafter cited in text as GDC with paragraph number.

[6] For a striking description of the evangelizing power of silent witness, see Pope Paul VI, *Evangelii Nuntiandi* 21 (1975). Online at www.vatican.va/holy_father/paul_vi /apost_exhortations/documents/hf_p-vi_exh_19751208_evangelii-nuntiandi_en.html.

[7] Pope Francis has written: "In virtue of their baptism, all the members of the People of God have become missionary disciples. . . . Every baptized Christian is a missionary to the extent that he or she has encountered the love of God in Christ Jesus; we no longer say that we are 'disciples' and 'missionaries', but rather that we are always 'missionary disciples'." *Evangelii Gaudium* 120. Online at www.vatican.va/evangelii-gaudium/en.

The third step in the church's mission is the formation of local Christian communities. This takes place through *initiatory activity*. The Rite of Christian Initiation of Adults (RCIA) is now a growing focus of that initiatory activity with adults.

Once a Christian community has been formed, the fourth step is *pastoral activity*, caring for ongoing formation in Christian living. There are elements of catechesis in each of these four steps of the church's mission. The form of mystagogy that is our focus fits into the fourth step, as part of the church's pastoral activity.

It was noted above that mystagogy falls within the larger framework of catechesis. That merits further consideration. Mystagogy is one form of liturgical catechesis, that itself is one among many other kinds of catechesis. Church documents speak of liturgical catechesis as "an eminent kind of catechesis" (GDC 71). Liturgical catechesis takes place in several phases:

- catechesis that prepares for celebration of the liturgy (RCIA and thereafter);
- catechesis that occurs within the celebration itself; and
- catechesis that follows after and flows from the celebration.

These three phases can be characterized as catechesis *for, through,* and *from* the liturgy.[8]

Phase two, catechesis *through* celebration of the liturgy, though it is not technically known as mystagogy, deserves further commentary. The *Catechism* (1074) calls the liturgy "the privileged place for catechizing the People of God." This means that the celebration of the liturgy, that is primarily worship of God, also nourishes faith (SC 33) and has an ongoing formative power as the liturgical year unfolds.[9] The *Catechism* (1075) teaches that the goal of liturgical catechesis is "to initiate people into the mystery of Christ. . . ." Initiation into the mystery of Christ is at the heart of catechesis, just as it is in the liturgy. That initiation begins in the liturgy, in the sacraments of initiation, and it continues

[8] Catherine Dooley adds a fourth phase, catechesis for mission, in "To Be What We Celebrate: Engaging the Practice of Liturgical Catechesis," *New Theology Review* 17, no. 4 (November 2004): 9–17.

[9] Consilium, *Universal Norms on the Liturgical Year and the Calendar* 1 (Vatican, 1969). This document can be found among the front materials in the 2010 *Roman Missal*.

in all subsequent celebrations of Eucharist and the other sacraments; it continues as well in post-sacramental mystagogical formation.

The liturgy itself can thus be said to be the beginning of mystagogy. How does that happen? Several aspects of the celebration help make that possible. First, if those who plan and lead the celebration are "thoroughly imbued with the spirit and power of the liturgy," they become models and teachers for the faithful (SC 14). Second, if the celebration "corresponds as aptly as possible to the needs, the preparation, and the culture of the participants,"[10] they will be able to enter into it more easily and make it their own. Third, the celebration will begin the process of opening up the symbols if they are both human and holy. That is, the symbols help people connect liturgy and life if they are shaped with loving care and bear the stamp of their maker's hand (i.e., they are human) and yet are "able to bear the weight of mystery, awe, reverence, wonder" (i.e., they are holy).[11] The symbols need to show both the traces of their origin in human rituals and the memory and imprint of how their meaning has been transformed through the saving actions of God in salvation history. Such symbols are "truly worthy, becoming, and beautiful, signs and symbols of the supernatural world" (SC 122). Fourth, a mystagogical turn of phrase in the words left to the presider's discretion, such as the homily, invitations, and brief introductions, can open up what the liturgy means for life. In ways such as these, the celebration itself can become an effective "first catechesis," the beginning of the formal mystagogy to follow.

The third and last phase of liturgical catechesis that is part of the ongoing formation of the community includes the mystagogy that is our focus. That is the catechesis that follows after and flows *from* liturgical celebration.[12]

---

[10] *General Instruction of the Roman Missal* 352 (ICEL translation, 2010), found among the front materials in the 2010 *Roman Missal*. Hereafter cited in text as GIRM with paragraph number.

[11] United States Conference of Catholic Bishops, *Built of Living Stones: Art, Architecture, and Worship* nos. 146–148 (Washington, DC: USCCB, 2000).

[12] The term "mystagogy" usually refers to the fourth period of the RCIA. Liturgical catechesis continues after initiation as part of the pastoral activity of continuing formation of the community that is named variously in GDC as "continuous education," "ongoing formation," "permanent catechesis" (51, 71). Although this ongoing liturgical catechesis, called "an eminent kind of catechesis," is described as both preparing for the sacraments

What is mystagogy? The origins of the word "mystagogy" help make that clear. In ancient Greek religious culture, mystagogy meant being guided into the mysteries (for example, the sacred religious rites of mythraic cults). The root words in Greek are *muein*, to close one's eyes/mouth, in a feeling of awe at the experience of those secret rites, and *ago*, to lead or guide. The experienced guide is called a mystagogue. Mystagogy is a kind of apprenticeship, a learning by doing. That is a natural human process still in use today—we learn to drive or to cook by doing it under the tutoring of a skilled driver or cook who can guide us in doing it and explain it to us more and more fully as we progress. The "it" in our context is initiation into the dying and rising of Jesus.

How does mystagogy work? After noting that the aim of liturgical catechesis is "to initiate people into the mystery of Christ," the *Catechism* adds "by proceeding from the visible to the invisible, from the sign to the thing signified, from the 'sacraments' to the mysteries" (1075). This is a simple, yet apt description.[13]

There are three steps in the process of mystagogy. The starting point is the experience of the liturgical signs and symbols used in the celebration. They have already communicated to us, without words, what it is that the sacrament accomplishes; they do the meaning. The words that accompany the ritual action give us a first articulation of what that meaning and effect are. This articulation, however, is not yet the fully stated meaning that formal mystagogical reflection will draw out.[14] Mystagogy thus proceeds from the visible to the invisible, from the liturgical signs to what they signify, from the sacraments to the mystery. That is the starting point for the formal mystagogy to come.

The next step, mystagogy proper, is the formal, structured process that helps people name and reflect on their liturgical experience. In keeping with the multilayered reality of symbols described earlier, that reflection can draw on the experience of the underlying human ritual,

---

and promoting a deeper understanding and experience of the liturgy (71), it implements what can be seen as an extension of the RCIA period of mystagogy. This book uses the term "mystagogy" in that extended sense.

[13] For commentary, see Catherine Dooley, "From the Visible to the Invisible: Mystagogy in the Catechism of the Catholic Church," *The Living Light* 31 (Spring 1995): 29–35.

[14] In fact, as ritual studies teach us, the meaning of ritual goes beyond what words can ever say about it. Ritual is its own way of knowing. See Ted W. Jennings, "On Ritual Knowledge," *Journal of Religion* 62 (1982): 111–127.

on what Scriptures and tradition tell us about the transformation of those rituals in Jewish life and especially in the life of Jesus and his early followers. It can draw on the words that accompany the ritual actions and on subsequent reflections within the Christian community to interpret the meaning of the rites. And above all, it invites people to connect those rituals to the paschal mystery of Christ.[15]

The final step in the mystagogical process is a mystagogy for mission, to guide people in inserting themselves into the Christ story and to ask what it means for Christian living. How are Christian lives to be shaped and formed into the pattern of Christ's living, dying, and rising, into a journey of dying to self and rising to a newness of life in him? Christians are sent from the Eucharist to live out that dying and rising in silent witness in the world,[16] and when they return from that mission to celebrate the Eucharist again, the cycle of liturgy and life repeats itself.

---

[15] The *Rite of Christian Initiation of Adults* 244 describes the period of mystagogy this way: "This is a time for the community and the neophytes to grow in their grasp of the paschal mystery and in making it part of their lives through meditation on the Gospel, and sharing in the Eucharist, and doing the works of charity." Note the parallel to RCIA 76, that calls for catechumens to be formed by teaching, community living, liturgical celebration, and leading lives of witness to the gospel. Again, it is learning by doing under wise explanatory guidance. GDC, 90–91 sets the baptismal catechumenate as the model for all the church's catechizing activity. The ongoing mystagogy we are concerned with should thus draw inspiration from the holistic mystagogy in the final period of the RCIA.

[16] In a lovely phrase, Paul says that we are "always carrying in the body the death of Jesus, so that the life of Jesus may also be made visible in our bodies" (2 Cor 4:10).

2

Procedures and Resources

A biblical paradigm

What kind of pastoral process is a conducive setting for effective mystagogy? The Scriptures provide us a wonderful example. Luke's story of the two disciples on the way to Emmaus on that first Easter Day (Luke 24:13–35) gives us a marvelous model for how mystagogy takes place.

> When he was at the table with them, he took bread, blessed and broke it, and gave it to them. Then their eyes were opened, and they recognized him; and he vanished from their sight. They said to each other, "Were not our hearts burning within us while he was talking to us on the road, while he was opening the scriptures to us?" That same hour they got up and returned to Jerusalem; and they found the eleven and their companions gathered together. They were saying, "The Lord has risen indeed, and he has appeared to Simon!" Then they told what had happened on the road, and how he had been made known to them in the breaking of the bread (30–35).

"Were not our hearts burning within us" is a beautiful example of mystagogy. The two disciples are now able to name what they had experienced. It starts with that experience, and so we need to retrace their journey. A week earlier they had come with Jesus to Jerusalem, where "they supposed that the kingdom of God was to appear immediately"

(Luke 19:11). Passover Week in Jerusalem followed the same pattern as the earlier phases of Jesus' public ministry. In each of the previous phases of his ministry in Luke's account (first in his home region of Galilee and then on the long teaching journey to Jerusalem), initial interest in his urgent message about the nearness of God's reign gave way to nonacceptance. In Jerusalem the pattern was repeated. Within a few short days, cries of "Hosanna" gave way to shouts of "Crucify him." When Jesus was arrested in the garden, Mark says, "All of them deserted him and fled" (14:50). Devastated by the death of Jesus, the two disciples left Jerusalem with their high hopes in tatters: "we had hoped that he was the one to redeem Israel" (Luke 24: 21). Their story ends in failure. It is told in the past tense, clearly implying that it is over. In telling it in this way, they are also saying that "they are ex-followers of a prophet, with left-over lives and nowhere to go but away."[1] When life feels like that, what other option is there? They have abruptly left Jerusalem and abandoned the band of disciples, dismayed and deeply distressed by what had happened the last few days.

The following scenes unfold quickly. The Stranger draws out their story with two simple questions: "What are you discussing?" and "What things?" (Luke 24:17, 19). After listening with respect to their soul-wrenching story, the Stranger gives it a new ending: "Was it not necessary that the Messiah should suffer these things and then enter into his glory?" (24:26). Jesus is a master catechist at work. He retells their story using their own biblical tradition, "beginning with Moses and all the prophets" (24:27); he retells it not as failure, but as glory. Doubly gifted by his respectful listening to their experience and his telling it in a new way, the two disciples offer hospitality and invite the Stranger to stay with them.

At table that evening the Stranger becomes their host, the disciples recognize who he is, and he vanishes before their eyes. In that moment Easter faith has dawned in their hearts; they have journeyed from complete loss of their great hopes and fragile incipient faith in him to full Easter faith. "Were not our hearts burning within us while he was talking to us on the road, while he was opening up the scriptures to us?"

---

[1] Denis McBride, *The Gospel of Like: A Reflective Commentary* (Northport, NY: Costello, 1982), 318.

(24:32). That is the moment of mystagogy for them; they can now name what they have experienced.[2]

In the strength of their newfound awareness that Jesus is alive, implying that they are still his disciples and that the mission he had entrusted to them earlier was still theirs, they return to Jerusalem with a mission to tell the others "what had happened on the road, and how he had been made known to them in the breaking of the bread" (24:35). What had prepared them for that moment of mystagogy and mission was their experience of the opening up of the Scriptures and the breaking of the bread—their story of the tragic events in Jerusalem was retold for them and reinterpreted through word and table.

There is a lesson here for us. Mystagogy of the Eucharist is not a purely intellectual exercise; it needs an experiential context. Liturgy alone is not enough. It is only one in a series of ministerial moments. It has to begin in the pastoral ministry of walking with the disciples— listening to the story they have to tell and then helping them to see it anew through the eyes of Scripture. These two moments of ministry can be seen as pastoral companioning and ministry of Word. That breaking open of life experience with the help of Scripture should reach full expression in the liturgy of the Word (in proclamation and homily), and in a third moment, the enactment of the Lord's Supper. Only then can the moments of mystagogy and mission unfold.

The lesson is this: a mystagogy of the Eucharist has a far better chance of being effective if we follow the Emmaus paradigm. The immediate context is the celebration of the Eucharist itself, a celebration in which the presence of the Risen Lord is "made known in the breaking of the bread." We need to read the Emmaus story backwards. The Lord's presence can best be made known when the actions of the holy meal, reminiscent of the best of our human meals, are performed with prayerful remembrance of how Jesus transformed sharing bread and wine into the memorial of his total self-giving in death. That, in turn, depends on a liturgy of the Word that opens up the participants' life experience in proclamation and homily so that the life stories of the gathered assembly are named in a new and deeper way. And that in turn depends on

---

[2] What they experienced was not just that the Scriptures had been opened up to their minds, but that their hearts had been set on fire. Mystagogy addresses the heart more than the head.

walking with the disciples to first learn what their stories are and how they embody a Jesus-like giving of self in love and service for others. Placed in that setting, mystagogy of the Eucharist can foster a growing and deeper commitment to live out the mission of Christian witness and to work for bringing about the reign of God in the world. So how can we approach that mystagogy?

Priorities and Procedures

An effective mystagogy for participants in the celebration of the Eucharist can be enhanced in a number of ways. Some practical recommendations gleaned from my experience follow.

- Provide liturgical celebrations that are as cared-for and prayerful as possible. The first pastoral priority and task in undertaking a mystagogy of the Eucharist is to ensure that the celebrations themselves and all the pastoral activity that precedes them have been carried out as effectively as possible over a period of time. This provides the rich foundational experience on which mystagogy can reflect.

- Plan an approach to mystagogy that capitalizes on the skills of the facilitator. In my experience, an interactive style is most likely to draw adults into the process. One of the basic principles of adult education is to involve participants in the process, so that they learn from their own experience as well as from the accumulated historical experience of the church.[3]

- In preparing for the session, facilitators should have versed themselves in the ritual actions, in their human and Christian roots, and in the array of meanings these actions can have. This allows the facilitator to help participants make connections between the liturgy and their daily lives. In addition to other available resources,

---

[3] NCCB, *Sharing the Light of Faith: National Catechetical Directory for Catholics of the United States*, places great stress on an experiential approach to catechesis (176.d) and directs "that adults should play a central role in their own education" (185.b). International Council for Catechesis, *Adult Catechesis in the Christian Community* (1992) stresses the "fundamental importance of the *dialogical* approach" (57, emphasis original). These documents can be found in *The Catechetical Documents: A Parish Resource* (Chicago: Liturgy Training Publications, 1996). See also GDC 172–176.

background briefings are included in the following chapters. Use of these resources best accomplishes the purpose of mystagogy if the goal is not imparting detailed technical information, but rather offering focused responses and reflection in the interactions with the participants. Flexibility in presenting this material is a skill that becomes an art with practice.

• Pay attention to the physical setting. Adult education theory underlines the value of a welcoming atmosphere. The traditional classroom configuration subtly suggests passive involvement to the participants. A circular configuration is more apt to encourage active participation.

• Create a hospitable environment through appropriate use of light, color, and symbols. The environment might also include enshrining one or more of the symbols used in the portion of the Eucharist to be reflected on in the session. In conjunction with this, religious educator Thomas Groome recommends using a focusing activity that also invites participants into a shared frame of mind, one of mutual respect and readiness to enter together into what the mystagogy will unfold.[4] A short prayer (e.g., an Our Father) is probably not enough to accomplish this.

• An effective way to begin the mystagogical session itself is asking participants to name all the ritual actions that comprise the portion of the Eucharist being reflected on. In the mystagogy of the early church, these ritual elements were named one by one and then broken open by the bishop or deacon who led the mystagogy. In light of the above principle for adult education, it would be best to involve the participants in the naming process through a series of questions. An alternate or complementary approach might be to have them relive that portion of the liturgy in memory and imagination at the outset of the session.[5]

---

[4] For a fuller discussion, see Thomas H. Groome, *Sharing Faith: A Comprehensive Approach to Religious Education and Pastoral Ministry* (HarperSanFrancisco, 1991), 155–174.

[5] Adult education theory currently stresses the role imagination plays in adult learning. See for example John Dirkx, "The Power of Feelings: Emotion, Imagination, and the Construction of Meaning in Adult Learning," in *The New Update on Adult Learning Theory*, edited by Sharan B. Merriam, 63–72 (San Francisco: Jossey-Bass, 2001). Engaging the imagination of the participants, however, can be taken a step beyond our human

- The two fundamental questions in mystagogy are: (1) what do we do? and (2) what does it mean? The reflection thus begins with naming and describing the ritual action before asking and reflecting on what it can mean.

- For the sake of participants who are visual learners, I have learned that it is good to use visual modes of presentation as well. PowerPoint or a similar technology is effective and not hard to master.

- Keep in mind these recommendations when creating a PowerPoint presentation:

  - Gold letters on a plain dark blue background is the most legible combination for the human eye. Backgrounds that are "busy" can distract viewers. This style can be applied to all PowerPoint slides at once or set up as a permanent style on a master format.

  - PowerPoint slides completely filled with script divide the attention of participants and distract them. Instead, insert text boxes that each contain a key word or a vital concept expressed in only a few words to capture the heart of what is being said orally. These boxes can be displayed one by one using the animation function, so that participants focus on each idea as it appears.

  - If a larger text is being posted in its entirety, it helps to format the text box with a lighter background color and to put the text in dark blue. Particular words or phrases can be highlighted sequentially by clicking on the insert function, choosing shapes, and then choosing the "line" shape to insert beneath select words/phrases. The line can be formatted for size and color, and animation (appear or wipe) can be added.

  - Images support interest and comprehension, and they provide overtones of meaning that words cannot capture completely. Images may also appeal better to viewers who are more image-driven than word-driven. A wealth of works of Christian art, from catacomb frescoes to apse mosaics to classical paintings and

---

imagining what the Eucharist means. William T. Cavanaugh, *Torture and Eucharist* (Malden, MA: Blackwell Publishers Inc., 1998), 279, writes these words worth pondering: "to participate in Eucharist is to live inside God's imagination." How can our human imagining be folded into that of God in mystagogy?

contemporary photos, is available on websites such as Wikimedia Commons and Google/images.[6]

* One final recommendation: be open to discovering what participants already know about Eucharist without ever having put it into words. I have learned to trust that participants already know more than I had expected. One of the delightful discoveries for them is to put words to their experiences for the first time—like the two disciples on the road. "Were not our hearts burning within us?" One of the great benefits of mystagogy is that it enables participants to name their own experience and to learn from it.

Reflective Resources

Helpful general resources for mystagogical reflection on the Eucharist include the following.

Baldovin, John F. *Bread of Life, Cup of Salvation: Understanding the Mass*. Come and See Series. Lanham, MD: Rowman & Littlefield, 2003.

Bernardin, Cardinal Joseph. *Guide for the Assembly*. Chicago: Liturgy Training Publications, 1997.

Bernier, Paul. *Living the Eucharist: Celebrating Its Rhythms in Our Lives*. Mystic, CT: Twenty-Third Publications, 2005.

Bernstein, Eleanor, ed. *Liturgical Gestures Words Objects*. Notre Dame, IN: Notre Dame Center for Pastoral Liturgy, 1995.

Boselli, Goffredo. *The Spiritual Meaning of the Liturgy: School of Prayer, Source of Life*. Translated by Barry Hudock. Collegeville, MN: Liturgical Press, 2014.

Donghi, Antonio. *Actions and Words: Symbolic Language and the Liturgy*. Collegeville, MN: Liturgical Press, 1997.

---

[6] In using images from the web, attribution to sources should be included in small print at the bottom of the slide. If the images are copyrighted, prior permission must be obtained. Many of the Google images are copyrighted, but the advanced search feature includes a "usage rights" option that enables one to limit search results to those images that may be reused and even modified. Images on Wikimedia Commons are not copyrighted. Copyrighting of images may vary on other websites such as: ATLA CDRI (Cooperative Digital Resources Initiative); EnVisionChurch Gallery of Images; Pitts Theology Library: Digital Image Archive.

Fischer, Balthasar. *Signs Words & Gestures: Short Homilies on the Liturgy.*
Translated by Matthew J. O'Connell. Collegeville, MN: Pueblo, 1981,
1990.

Kelly, Tony. *The Bread of God: Nurturing a Eucharistic Imagination.* Liguori,
MO: Liguori, 2001.

Koester, Anne Y. *Sunday Mass: Our Role and Why It Matters.* Collegeville,
MN: Liturgical Press, 2007.

Mahony, Cardinal Roger. *Gather Faithfully Together: Guide for Sunday Mass.*
Chicago: Liturgy Training Publications, 1997.

Mitchell, Nathan, ed. *Table Bread and Cup: Meditations on Eucharist.* Notre
Dame, IN: Notre Dame Center for Pastoral Liturgy, 2000.

Turner, Paul. *At the Supper of the Lamb: A Pastoral and Theological
Commentary on the Mass.* Chicago: Liturgy Training Publications, 2011.

Turner, Paul. *Companion to the Roman Missal.* Chicago: World Library
Publications, 2011.

Part II

Mystagogy of the Eucharist

3

Gathering

We turn now to the reflective walk-through of the Eucharist. This chapter and those that follow will each focus on one segment of the Eucharist[1] and they will use the following format for each segment of the mystagogy:

- introduction
- background briefing on ritual symbols and their meaning[2]
- outline of the mystagogy session, including:[3]
  - sample starter questions (in italics) to frame the session
  - sample themes for interactive reflection[4]
  - sample titles for PowerPoint slides
  - sample texts for PowerPoint slides
  - sample visuals for the PowerPoint
- reflective resources

[1] Depending on the goals, participants, and available time for the mystagogical reflection, the segments can be used in several ways: in individual sessions, in combinations (e.g., gathering and word, presentation of gifts and eucharistic prayer, communion and sending), or combined into one longer session.

[2] These briefings are not meant to be the actual presentations. They simply provide background information and ideas for the facilitator, who may have other resource materials and experience to draw on as well.

[3] These items are labeled "sample" to give facilitators some leads. I encourage facilitators to develop items of their own that suit their perspectives and style. The mystagogy benefits greatly from facilitator ownership and personal enthusiasm. Texts in square brackets [ ] in the tables are hints and instructions for the facilitator.

[4] This and the next three items are presented in tables for PowerPoint slides related to the starter questions. The sequence of inserting texts and visuals is sometimes inverted for the sake of unfolding the meaning.

In its most basic form, mystagogy starts from the liturgical action/ symbols and asks participants to name and reflect on it with two questions: What do we do? What does it mean?

This is a dual process of naming the ritual actions and their symbols and reflecting on them. Use of visuals and an interactive conversational approach are highly recommended. Such a mystagogical approach solicits the responses of participants and explores the meaning of the ritual actions with the help of their experiences, both of daily human rituals and liturgical rituals, and of various kinds of texts, such as the prayers of the rite, what church documents and other commentaries have said, and occasional poetic reflections.

Introduction

The introductory rites of the Mass consist of the following ritual elements:

- entrance procession
- reverence of the altar and greeting
- penitential act
- Gloria
- opening prayer

The mystagogy for this session will focus on the first two elements.

Background Briefing[5]

Gathering

The Introductory rites serve as an introduction and preparation for the Mass. Their purpose is to "ensure that the faithful, who come together as one, establish communion and dispose themselves properly to listen to the Word of God and to celebrate the Eucharist worthily" (GIRM 46). Celebration of the Mass begins officially with the entrance

---

[5] These briefings expand on what I have written earlier: "A Mystagogy of the Eucharist," *Liturgical Ministry* 20, no. 4 (Fall 2011): 161–166. Ideas repeated here, copyrighted by the author, are used with permission of the publisher and will not be footnoted.

procession. But something has gone before. The procession begins only "when the people are gathered" (GIRM 47). What is that gathering that has already taken place and what does it mean? To gather is to

> be summoned
> by someone
> to do something
> together.

Each of these phrases merits reflection. The Latin name for the church (*ecclesia*) is actually a transliteration of a Greek word that means those duly summoned for an assembly, a public convocation. Thus to gather together is to "be church." The church building is simply the meeting place for the church, the house of the church. The one who summons us together is God. That call has come to us in so many ways—in baptism, in faith formation, through the example of family and friends, when the day and hour for gathering approaches, when we hear the church bells, or when someone says, "It's time to go." What we are to do when we are assembled is to listen and respond to God's word and to share a holy meal. And this is something we do together, as a holy people summoned by God. God calls us as a people.

When does Mass actually begin for people? They answer that question in many ways. For example: when they spend time with the Scripture readings before Sunday, or when they dress and get themselves ready on Sunday morning, or when they arrive at church and are greeted by ministers of hospitality and other members of the community, or when they settle into their pews for a moment of quiet prayer, or when the entrance song begins, or when their spirits finally quiet down and they really listen to the readings. The list of examples goes on.

The coming together is a journey, a pilgrimage to the place of worship. We come from home and family, from colleagues and workplaces of the previous week, from all walks of life. We bring with us all we have experienced since our last gathering—sickness, health, success, failures, friendships strengthened, relationships broken, worries and concerns, disappointments, dreams, and hopes. We bring our lives, ourselves, our world. All this we carry with us as we stream toward the gathering place. We can think of our coming together for Mass as an informal entrance procession, a great streaming together of people that is the prelude to the formal ritual procession. We are the vanguard of that solemn entrance procession. "So this is the entrance procession, coming from all directions, made up of all ages, several races, a variety of economic circumstances and political outlooks—and speaking at least three first languages! But all are in a great procession, assembling in the house of the Church. 'We shall go up with joy.'"[6]

Entrance procession

The Mass officially begins with the formal entrance procession. What is a procession? A poet puts it this way:

> What is procession?
> Movement from place to place,
> measured movement, stately movement,
> a representative few treading a representative distance:
> journey distilled.
> This is what all journeys are, it proclaims,
> this is journey at its heart.
> Again and again,
> from week to week,
> from age to age,
> there is something of endings and beginnings;
> of closing doors behind and opening those ahead,
> of meeting and walking together.

> What is procession? A journey, distilled.

> From age to age, from east to west
> we have skipped and limped and marched and run
> and shuffled and strolled our various ways.
> Our stories reverberate in measured tread.

> From age to age, from east to west,
> our hurried feet have marked
> the peaks and valleys, the sand and stone,
> the mud, the grass, the dust,
> the streams.

---

[6] Cardinal Roger Mahony, *Gather Faithfully Together: Guide for Sunday Mass* (Chicago: Liturgy Training Publications, 1997), 43.

We pause now in solemn pace to remember:
All ground is holy ground.
We come interiorly shoeless.

What is procession?
It is journey distilled—journey at its heart,
a gathering into one movement
of a Church on the way:
a pilgrim people, a dusty, longing people,
yet walking with heads high;
knowing ourselves, showing ourselves
to be the royal nation, the holy people
won by the Son,
called by his Word,
gathered around his table.
There we discover again,
from age to age, from east to west,
for all our journeys,
the source, the ground, the companion, the way.[7]

What lovely phrases: "a representative few treading a representative distance," "journey distilled," "journey at its heart." The ministers entering in procession march in our stead. As we watch, the procession invites us all to march with them in spirit, to enter onto this holy ground "interiorly shoeless."

So the entrance procession is different from a crowd of people walking along a street, or a parade. But what makes it different? To answer that we need to ask other questions: how do the ministers carry themselves as they walk and what ritual actions do they perform as they walk along in the procession? A processional cross lifted high and flanked by two candles leads the procession. Then comes a minister of the Word holding the Book of the Gospels aloft, followed by the deacon and presider. Why are cross, candles, and the Book of the Gospels carried in through the midst of the assembly in solemn procession? What do they tell us about ourselves and the celebration that is to follow?

---

[7] Janet Schlichting, OP, "Processing," in *Liturgical Gestures Words Objects*, ed. Eleanor Bernstein, 8 (Notre Dame, IN: Notre Dame Center for Pastoral Liturgy, 1995). Hereafter cited as LGWO.

Processional cross

What story does the cross tell? In answer to that question, people have no trouble in identifying that the cross tells the story of Jesus' death and resurrection. It tells of the moment when he offered himself completely for our salvation, a self-offering that God accepted by raising him from the dead. Christ's death on the cross, however, was not an isolated action. His journey of self-giving began with the incarnation, when he

> emptied himself,
> taking the form of a slave,
> being born in human likeness. (Phil 2:7)

That process of self-giving continued during his public ministry. Jesus taught us in words, parables, and deeds how we are to accept and treat one another, to give ourselves in serving others in their needs, to set self aside and forgive. He bequeathed that way of life to us in the great commandment of love and in his Last Supper commands to "do this in remembrance of me" (Luke 22:19)[8] and to "wash one another's feet" (John 13:14). His life of self-emptying reached its final and fullest expression when

> he humbled himself
> and became obedient to the point of death—
> even death on a cross. (Phil 2:8)

How does the processional cross tell that story? History has left us many images of the cross. Some of the earliest are found in the catacombs, where the cross sometimes takes the shape of a Chi Ro (*chr* in English, the first two letters of the name "Christ" in Greek) or where it becomes the standard for a pennant or a laurel crown of victory.[9] That same theme of victory became more explicit in the fourth century when St. Helena discovered the true cross in Jerusalem. A cross encrusted with jewels quickly became a common image in apse mosaics of Christian

---

[8] Jesus' words over the bread and cup named in advance the saving meaning of his death. We'll come to those words in chapter 6.

[9] This way of "disguising" the cross may have been an early attempt to avoid derision over the scandal of the founder of Christianity having been executed as a common criminal.

churches, for example in Santa Pudenziana in Rome (384–399 CE).[10] Later the death of Christ was depicted, in words and images, as falling asleep on the wood of the cross. The Gero Crucifix in Cologne Cathedral (c. 965–970 CE) presents such an image. There is an air of peacefulness about the figure of Christ. Another reading of his death can be found in a cross (c. 1230 CE) in the National Gallery of Umbria in Perugia, Italy. In this portrayal, Christ's arms are freed from the cross and reach down to invite viewers into an embrace of love.

History has left other images telling a more graphic story of suffering and death. Think of the gaunt and emaciated figure on the "plague" crosses, such as the one in Cologne (1301 CE). It was believed to have curative power (like the Cristo Negro crucifix in Chimayo, New Mexico), and it became a popular place of pilgrimage and prayer in the mid-fourteenth century for those seeking healing during the time of the Black Death. People of that time saw their own suffering in the gaunt emaciated figure of the Crucified One. Or think of the Isenheim Altarpiece (c. 1510–1515 CE), attributed to Matthäus Grünewald. The flesh of Christ is putrid-looking, his hands and extremities twisted in agony. Placed above an altar in the chapel of an Alsatian leprosarium, it invited patients not so much to reflect on the Mass celebrated there but to identify with Christ in their own disfigurement and suffering. Think, too, of the realistic images of the scourged and crucified Christ still found in so many of the countries brought into Christianity by Spanish missionaries. In these familiar and beloved images, people see the suffering of Christ that is played out in their own lives. They love another kind of image as well—a cross on which stories and scenes of their daily lives and work are painted.

So what other stories do these crosses tell? Christ said that any who wanted to become his disciples should "take up their cross" and follow him (Matt 16:24). There are so many ways, both large and small, in which we die to sin and self and rise to newness of life day by day. The history of the world, says Karl Rahner, is a terrible and sublime history of dying and rising that reached its fulfillment in the dying and rising

---

[10] Santa Pudenziana, one of the earliest churches in Rome, was built over the site of an early house church. Its fourth-century apse mosaic, poorly restored in the sixteenth century, shows Christ clothed in purple and seated, an artistic convention used for magistrates and teachers. In the background the skyline of Jerusalem at that time is clearly recognizable, and mounted on a hilltop (Calvary) stands a large, jewel-encrusted cross.

of Christ,[11] to which we are all called to join our daily moments of dying and rising. The cross carried in the entrance procession tells the story of Jesus. It also sums up that liturgy of daily dying and rising that we all bring into the assembly. It tells our story too.

Candles

What story do the candles tell? In this era of electric lights, candles have lost much of their practical use. We use candles most commonly to create a desired atmosphere by the soft glow and subtle scent they spread, or perhaps to provide a focal point for centering prayer. At an earlier time, and even in power outages now, candles have also served to cast a little light to help us find our way in the darkness and also to give off a little warmth on cold winter days. As the wick burns down, candles melt and are consumed in the process; they readily serve as an image of dying, of serving at their own expense.

When asked what is *the* candle for Christians, people readily answer that it is the paschal candle. We light it during the Easter Vigil. As that candle's light passes from taper to taper, the church where we are assembled gradually glows brighter and brighter with its light, a light that dances on our faces. That tells us that along with Christ we too become the light of the world. At what other times is the paschal candle used? People can also name these. We use it throughout the Easter season and at every baptism and funeral. Its light marks the beginning and end of our lives as disciples of Christ. Jesus said, "I am the light of the world. Whoever follows me will never walk in darkness but will have the light of life" (John 8:12). He also said to his disciples: "You are the light of the world" (Matt 5:14). He taught them that their light is not to be hidden away but to be put on a lampstand and to shine before others, "so that they may see your good works and give glory to your Father in heaven" (Matt 5:15–16). The candles in the entrance procession remind us of Christ in whom we have become light for the world. However dimly or brightly our light has burned that week, the candles are the symbols of the good works, the warmth and witness we have brought into the lives of others as we spent something of ourselves in loving service.

---

[11] Karl Rahner calls that the "liturgy of the world" in his article "Considerations on the Active Role of the Person in the Sacramental Event," in *Theological Investigations* XIV, translated by David Bourke, 161–184 (New York: Seabury, 1976). We will return to this idea in chapter 8.

Book of the Gospels

Whose story does the Book of the Gospels tell? The answer is in the narrative pattern and story line of the Gospels.[12] They tell the story of the life, words, deeds, death, and resurrection of Jesus. He is the pioneer, the pathfinder of faith, and he has brought it to completion (Heb 12:2). That is the path his disciples are to follow. The Gospel tells the story we espouse as our own, willing to follow in his footsteps and to lose our lives in loving service to others "for my sake and the sake of the gospel" (Mark 8:34). The Book of the Gospels carried in solemn procession tells our story too. The GIRM notes that "[i]t is a praiseworthy practice for the *Book of the Gospels* to be placed on the altar" (GIRM 122). There will be fuller reflections about the Book of the Gospels in chapter 4.

Reverencing the altar and greeting

The entrance procession through the midst of the assembly reaches its final destination at the altar table. This most noble of tables stands before the assembly as "a sign of Christ himself" (*Rite of Dedication of an Altar* 4). The presider reverences the altar table with a kiss in the name of the entire assembly. The altar is also a symbol that reminds us of what we ourselves are. "Since Christ, Head and Teacher, is the true altar, his members and disciples are also the spiritual altars on which the sacrifice of a holy life is offered to God" (*Rite of Dedication of an Altar* 2). That is why we have come at God's summons, to hear God's Word, and to offer a holy sacrifice with Christ in the power of the Spirit. The opening ritual dialogue of the Mass puts that into words: "In the name of the Father and of the Son and of the Holy Spirit" proclaims the presider, in words reminiscent of our baptism, claiming us for God as church, the assembly of God's holy people. To that we answer, "Amen." So be it. This is the first word spoken by the assembly. It will be repeated again and again throughout the celebration. "Amen" will be the focus of reflection in the final chapter.

In sum

The meaning the eucharistic gathering has for our lives is beautifully summed up in these simple yet solemn entrance rituals. We gather

---

[12] A more condensed form is found in the proclamation of the kerygma in Acts and in brief creedal statements in the epistles.

bringing the stories of our daily dying and rising in holy lives lived in imitation of Christ. We gather to hear them retold in the Gospel story that Jesus told about the reign of God and to which we are to give witness by our lives. We gather to place our lives and ourselves on the altar table to be offered in union with Christ's self-giving. The concluding rites will send us back into the world to continue to live out what we have come to celebrate.[13] The pastoral goal of this recurring lifelong cycle of life-liturgy-life is to continue and deepen what began in our baptism, initiation "into the mystery of Christ" (CCC 1075).

The Mystagogy

Setting the stage

The environment for this session could feature the community's processional cross mounted in its stand and flanked by candles.[14] Inviting participants to approach and venerate the cross by touch or bow would be fitting as part of the opening prayer/focus activity. This could also be done, either when appropriate during the session or at the conclusion of the reflective walk-through. Passing around a handheld crucifix for people to touch or kiss in silence could be another focusing activity.[15]

Table 3A

Topic slide for PowerPoint[16]	
Title	Gathering
Visual	assembly (local community)

---

[13] The themes anticipated in the gathering rite will be explored more fully in the chapters that follow.

[14] If this session is combined with the next one, on the Liturgy of the Word, it would be appropriate to enshrine the Book of the Gospels as well.

[15] Such acts would recall to mind the Veneration of the Cross on Good Friday and associate them with it.

[16] The material in the tables is offered as a resource. The cells (rows) between darker lines in each table, here and hereafter, represent sample individual PowerPoint slides. The mystagogy can be conducted without the PowerPoint slides, using only the starter questions and live interaction, if the facilitator so wishes.

Attending to experience

- *What do we do as part of the entrance rites?*

Table 3B

Elicit the elements in detail

- *In a moment of silence, remember and relive those things.*
- *Name aloud the elements of the entrance rites you love the most.*
- *Which elements help you best to enter into the celebration?*

Reflection on the ritual actions and symbols

Gathering

- *When does the celebration begin for you?*
- *Are there things you do before Mass to help you get ready?*
- *What does it feel like to gather together with others?*
- *What is gathering?*
- *What or who summons us for the liturgy?*

Table 3C

Themes	gathering gathering as unofficial procession
Title	Gathering
Visual	local community streaming toward entrance
Texts	[animate these phrases to appear one by one for open discussion] summoned by someone to do something together
Title	Gathering
Visual	local community streaming toward entrance [reduced size]
Text #1	Mahony quote [insert entire quote, underline following phrase] "all are in a great procession"

Entrance procession

- *What is procession?*
- *How is it different from walking down a crowded street? from a parade?*
- *What makes it different?*

Table 3D

Themes	final ritual moment of the gathering "representative few"—all walk in spirit Christian life: "journey distilled"
Title	Entrance procession
Visual	entrance procession of local community, showing cross, candles, book
Text	What is a procession?
Text #2	"Processing" [read, inserting favorite phrases one by one, e.g.,:] "representative few" "journey distilled" "holy ground" "we come interiorly shoeless"

- *How do the ministers carry themselves as they walk in the procession?*
- *What ritual actions do the ministers perform as they walk in the procession?*

Table 3E

Title	Procession
Texts	What do we do? [elicit the actions/objects in detail]
Visuals	processional cross close-up candle flame(s) close-up Book of the Gospels close-up
Text	What does this mean?

- *Why are cross, candles, and Book of the Gospels carried in through the midst of the assembly in solemn procession?*
- *What do these items tell us about ourselves and the celebration that is to follow?*

Processional cross

- *What story does the processional cross tell?*
- *How does the cross tell that story?*

Table 3F

Themes	story of Christ's death and resurrection culmination of his life of self-giving historical forms: disguised; victory; sleep; suffering and death
Title	Processional cross
Visual	processional cross close-up (local community's)
Text	What story does it tell?
Text #3	"even death on a cross" (Phil 2:8)
Title	How is that story told?
Text	*as victory*
Visuals	apse mosaics: St. Pudenziana (384–399) or St. Apollinare in Classe (sixth century)
Title	*. . . or as the sleep of death*
Visuals	Gero crucifix, full figure and close-up
Text	Gero Crucifix (c. 970)
Title	*. . . or as suffering and agony*
Visuals	plague cross (early 1300s), full figure and close-up
Text	What other stories does it tell? [favorite during Black Death]

- *What other stories does this cross tell?*
- *What did Jesus say to those who wanted to follow him?*

Table 3G

Themes	"take up your cross" daily dying to self (Paul)
Title	What other stories?
Visual	plague cross or a realistic crucifix [style favored by sufferers]
Text	"take up your cross" (Matt 16:24)

Visual	Isenheim Altarpiece [full screen]
Text	Isenheim Altarpiece (c. 1510–1515)
Visuals	Isenheim Altarpiece close-ups: hand, head and upper torso, head
Visual	crucifix by Graham Sutherland
Text	Graham Sutherland (1946) [holocaust image]

- *What does the processional cross tell us about Christian life?*

Table 3H

Title	? [big question mark, centered]
Texts	What other stories ought the cross be able to tell us today?

Candles

- *What story do candles tell?*
- *What is the candle for Christians?*

Table 3I

Themes	"I am the light of the world" "You are the light of the world" light in darkness, warmth = witness, charity
Title	Candles
Visual	several candle flames
Text	What story do they tell?
Visual	paschal candle
Text	"I am the light of the world" (John 8:12)
Visual	paschal candle at font with someone holding baptismal candle

- *What did Christ say to his disciples about the light of the world?*
- *What do the candles tell us about Christian life?*

Table 3J

Visuals	paschal candle [solitary image, centered] Easter Vigil tapers lighting up assembly [overlaid, full screen]
Text	"You are the light of the world" (Matt 5:14) [text in light color superimposed on visual]

Book of the Gospels

- *Whose story does the Book of the Gospels tell?*
- *What other stories does it tell?*

Table 3K

Themes	story disciples are to live out story of words, deeds, life, death of Jesus
Title	Book
Visual	Gospel Book in procession (local community)
Texts #4	"Book" [read entire poem, inserting the following:] "The dance is rigid down the aisle, a book embraced, held high, held dear" "the kernel of ourselves"

- *What do you think placing the Book of the Gospels on the altar means?*
- *What does the Book of the Gospels tell us about Christian life?*

Reverencing the altar

- *Why do the ministers bow to the altar?*
- *Why does the presider kiss the altar?*
- *What does reverencing the altar tell us about Christian life?*

Greeting the assembly

- *What is the first ritual action we do in the assembly?*
- *What does the sign of the cross tell us?*

Table 3L

Themes	Reminder of baptism "in name of" = belong to
Visual	people signing themselves (local community)
Text #5	"Sign of the Cross" [read poem, then insert text below]
Text	we belong to the Holy Trinity

- *What is the first word we say in the assembly?*
- *What does it mean?*

Table 3M

Themes	"so be it"—affirmation and commitment
Text #6	"Amen" [read poem, then insert final line] "Be careful when you say 'Amen.'"

- *At what other times in the Mass do we say "Amen"?*
- *What does the greeting tell us about Christian life?*

Recap slide

Table 3N

Theme	symbolic preview of the liturgy to follow and its meaning
Title	Gathering
Visuals	processional cross close-up, paschal candle, Gospel Book
Texts	procession: "journey distilled" symbols: "story condensed"

Texts

#1—Gathering[17]

"So this is the entrance procession, coming from all directions, made up of all ages, several races, a variety of economic circumstances and political outlooks—and speaking at least three first languages!

[17] Cardinal Mahony, *Guide for Sunday Mass*, no. 43.

But all are in a great procession, assembling in the house of the Church. 'We shall go up with joy'." (Cardinal Mahony, *Guide for Sunday Mass*, 43)

#2—"Processing," by Janet Schlichting, OP (LGWO, 8)

What is procession?
Movement from place to place,
measured movement, stately movement,
a representative few treading a representative distance:
journey distilled.
This is what all journeys are, it proclaims,
this is journey at its heart.

Again and again,
from week to week,
from age to age,
there is something of endings and beginnings;
of closing doors behind and opening those ahead,
of meeting and walking together.

What is procession? A journey, distilled.

From age to age, from east to west
we have skipped and limped and marched and run
and shuffled and strolled our various ways.
Our stories reverberate in measured tread.

From age to age, from east to west,
our hurried feet have marked
the peaks and valleys, the sand and stone,
the mud, the grass, the dust,
the streams.
We pause now in solemn pace to remember:
All ground is holy ground.
We come interiorly shoeless.

What is procession?
It is journey distilled—journey at its heart,
a gathering into one movement
of a Church on the way:
a pilgrim people, a dusty, longing people,

yet walking with heads high;
knowing ourselves, showing ourselves
to be the royal nation, the holy people
won by the Son,
called by his Word,
gathered around his table.
There we discover again,
from age to age, from east to west,
for all our journeys,
the source, the ground, the companion, the way.

#3—Phil 2:8

"he humbled himself
and became obedient to the point of death –
even death on a cross."

#4—"Book," by Gabe Huck (LGWO, 45)

The dance is rigid down the aisle,
a book embraced, held high, held dear:
the common carrier of the tales
on fiber come from cotton fields
and pulp from forest cut in Maine.
What earth has given hands have made
flat, thin and bound between two boards,
the pages covered now with marks
that image sounds that image all:
the pictures of pictures only
are letters gathered into words
and words lined up and bundled, tied—
yet here's the kernel of ourselves:
the poems, geneologies,
laws, letters, sayings, prophecies,
psalms, stories, visions handed on
from mouth to mouth and tongue to tongue
and page to page: a year or three
to tell it round again, this book
that dances now in incense sweet
and sweet its alphabet to kiss.

#5—"Sign of the Cross," by Mark Searle (LGWO, 9)

At the beginning and end of this Mass
at the beginning and end of our lives;
at the beginning and ending of all we do
stands the sign of the cross, saying:
this place, this space of time, this life,
this child, these people, this corpse,
belongs to the Lord and will not be
snatched from Him
who bears indelibly in his body
the marks of that same cross.

#6—"Amen," by Barbara Schmich (LGWO, 30)

Be careful of simple words said often.

"Amen" makes demands
like an unrelenting schoolmaster:
fierce attention to all that is said;
no apathy, no preoccupation, no prejudice permitted.
"Amen": We are present. We are open.
      We hearken. We understand.
      Here we are, we are listening to your word.
"Amen" makes demands
like a signature on a dotted line:
sober bond to all that goes before,
no hesitation, no half-heartedness, no mental
reservation allowed.

"Amen": We support. We approve.
      We are of one mind. We promise.
      May this come to pass. So be it.

Be careful when you say "Amen."

Reflective Resources

Bernardin, Cardinal Joseph. *Guide for the Assembly*, 7–10. Chicago: Liturgy Training Publications, 1997.

Bernstein, Eleanor, ed. *Liturgical Gestures Words Objects*. Notre Dame, IN: Notre Dame Center for Pastoral Liturgy, 1995.

Guardini, Romano. "The Sign of the Cross," cited in *How Firm a Foundation: Voices of the Early Liturgical Movement*, compiled and edited by Kathleen Hughes, 114. Chicago: Liturgy Training Publications, 1990.

Koester, Anne Y. *Sunday Mass: Our Role and Why It Matters*, 19–27. Collegeville, MN: Liturgical Press, 2007.

Mahony, Cardinal Roger. *Gather Together Faithfully: Guide for Sunday Mass*, 13–17. Chicago: Liturgy Training Publications, 1997.

Mitchell, Nathan, ed. *Table Bread and Cup: Meditations on Eucharist*, 1–5. Notre Dame, IN: Notre Dame Center for Pastoral Liturgy, 2000.

Ramshaw, Gail. *Words around the Table*. Chicago: Liturgy Training Publications, 1991.

Worship Office of the Archdiocese of Cincinnati. *We Gather in Christ: Our Identity as Assembly*. Chicago: Liturgy Training Publications, 1996.

Interlude

We now come to the core of the eucharistic celebration—the Liturgy of the Word and the Liturgy of the Eucharist. Origins of the Eucharist can be traced back to the beginnings of the church. The biblical accounts of the Last Supper (Matt 26:26–28; Mark 14:22–25; Luke 22:19–20; 1 Cor 11:23–25) describe the traditional Jewish table rituals Jesus performed over bread and wine. In a summary description of the communal life of the early community, Luke–Acts writes: "they devoted themselves to the apostles' teaching and fellowship, to the breaking of bread and the prayers" (Acts 2:42). This passage names four activities that express the unifying actions to which the Jerusalem community devoted itself. One might see in this idyllic description a faint foreshadowing of what would become a full-blown eucharistic rite: word and table, with the people's prayers of intercession.

In an account written about 150 CE, St. Justin the Martyr records just such a fuller description of how Sunday Eucharist was celebrated in the Church of Rome. Discovering this account is a breathtaking moment for people. It reads:

> On the day named after the sun, all who live in city or countryside assemble. The memoirs of the apostles or the writings of the prophets are read for as long as time allows. When the lector has finished, the president addresses us and exhorts us to imitate the splendid things we have heard. Then we all stand to pray. As we said earlier, when we have finished praying, bread, wine, and water are brought up. The president then prays and gives thanks according to his ability, and the people give their assent with an "Amen!" Next, the gifts over which the thanksgiving has been spoken are distributed, and everyone shares in them, while they are also sent via the deacons to the absent brethren. The wealthy who are willing make contributions, each

as he pleases, and the collection is deposited with the president, who aids orphans and widows, those who are in want because of sickness or some other reason, those in prison, and visiting strangers—in short, he takes care of all in need.[1]

When people hear this account from the early Church of Rome, they immediately recognize the pattern of our Sunday celebration. They can be asked to name these as the reading progresses. We sense with awe our own continuity with what the people of God have done throughout history. It is to this ancient rite of Word and Eucharist that we now turn.

---

[1] Justin the Martyr, *Apology* I:67, cited in Lucien Deiss, *Springtime of the Liturgy*, trans. Matthew J. O'Connell, 93–94 (Collegeville, MN: Liturgical Press, 1979). Scholars note that the word for "president" (*praeest*) in the original means "one who is over, who directs, who is the head of."

4

Proclaiming, Listening, Responding to the Word

Introduction

The Liturgy of the Word on Sundays consists of the following ritual elements:

- first reading
- responsorial psalm
- second reading
- acclamation before the Gospel (Alleluia)
- Gospel
- acclamation after the Gospel ("Praise to you . . .")
- homily
- profession of faith
- universal prayer

The mystagogy for this session will focus mostly on the ritual actions connected with the readings, especially the Gospel.

Background Briefing

GIRM 55 describes the structure and purpose of the Liturgy of the Word, stating that

in the readings, as explained by the Homily, God speaks to his
people, opening up to them the mystery of redemption and salvation, and offering spiritual nourishment; and Christ himself is
present through his word in the midst of the faithful. By silence
and by singing, the people make this divine word their own, and
affirm their adherence to it by means of the profession of faith; finally, having been nourished by the divine word, the people pour
out their petitions by means of the universal prayer for the needs
of the whole church and for the salvation of the whole world.

In simpler terms, this part of the Mass consists of proclaiming, listening
to, and responding to the word of God. That is the core of the Liturgy
of the Word. It is an extended experience of address and response, of
call and response. This dynamic is part and parcel of all human life
and interaction with others. The same is true of the dialogue with God
that takes place in the Liturgy of the Word. One might compare it to
human conversation.[1] We use words to express ideas, feelings, hopes
and dreams, to reply to them, and to set an appropriate course of action
for the future. In human conversations words are addressed not only
to the head but also and at times especially to the heart. That is why
they are often accompanied by gaze, facial expressions, gestures, bodily
postures, and touch—all forms of nonverbal communication that add a
meaningfulness of their own to the words. Indeed, nonverbal expressions
such as these "say" what words cannot say. Our conversations are also
punctuated by sentences left unfinished and moments of silence that
can be so expressive of what is beyond words. Conversation with God
in the Liturgy of the Word is marked by those same qualities—words
of address and response, bodily postures and gestures, and moments of
thoughtful silence. Further reflections are in order.

Shape of the Liturgy of the Word

First, a word about the *overall pattern* of the Liturgy of the Word. It
is an extended dialogue of call and response between God and us. How

---

[1] We should note one significant difference. In the biblical context, the "conversation"
between God and us can more aptly be named call and response. God's revelation comes
to us as a call. It calls us to respond to what God has in mind for how we are to live. Prayer
has often been compared to conversing with God, but it always starts with listening to
hear what God wants of us, to hear God's call. It is to that call that we are to respond.

do we know that God is speaking to us in the readings? Faith tells us that the words of Scripture have been inspired by God. The liturgy also tells us that over and over. The ritual dialogues surrounding the readings tell us these are not just our words but God's. "The Word of the Lord. / Thanks be to God." "Glory to you, O Lord." "The Gospel of the Lord. / Praise to you, Lord Jesus Christ." It is God who is speaking to us in the readings, not the lector who proclaims them. There is also a larger dialogic exchange. To God's word proclaimed in the entire set of readings and opened up in the homily, we respond by professing our faith and praying for the needs of our church and the world. That is actually a twofold response. In the creed we accept in faith what God has said, and in the universal prayer we carry out part of our mission, praying that God's reign may come in the church and the world. The Scriptures reveal to us something of God's saving plan and what God has done and continues to do to carry it out.

Proclamation

Next, let us look more closely at some of the elements. The words of Scripture are *proclaimed*. That verb comes from the Latin roots *pro + clamare*, that means to cry out, to shout forth. It is the solemn voice of a town crier, a herald announcing important news from a rooftop or from the front steps of a building in a public square in ancient times, or the cardinal protodeacon announcing the election of a new pope from the balcony of St. Peter's. It is different from the nervous, uninflected declamation of a poem or an historic speech of Lincoln or Martin Luther King, Jr., by a grade-schooler, or a matter-of-fact classroom lecture, or the sound of ordinary speech. The very tone and style of the proclamation tell us that this is special speech, that it is God's Word. We sit for the first two readings to mirror an attitude of receptivity to God's Word being proclaimed to us. The noble beauty of the ambo, the solemn grace of the lectors' mini-procession to it, and their posture at it all say the same. All this places demands on the preparation of lectors for their ministry.[2]

---

[2] For helpful ideas, see James A. Wallace, *The Ministry of Lectors*, second edition (Collegeville, MN: Liturgical Press, 2004).

Listening

Listening to the proclamation of the Scriptures is also different from the listening we do in everyday life. Our daily experience of listening presents us with a huge liturgical challenge. Cardinal Bernardin has written that "listening is a skill that grows dull in the barrage of words one hears all day long." Bombarded by talk radio and TV, by the cell phone conversations that surround us on streets and city busses, by the Muzak heard everywhere, we have learned to tune out the sounds around us. All this white noise weakens our desire to attend to what we're hearing; we simply turn off our ears. But attentive listening is a lost skill we can relearn. Bernardin continues: "In the liturgy we are schooled in the art of listening." In the liturgy we can learn again to listen and then carry that art over into daily life. It teaches us how to "be good listeners to one another, to the Lord, to the world with all its needs."[3]

How can the Liturgy of the Word help us relearn that art? Being good listeners requires us to practice a different kind of listening. In the prologue to his Rule for Benedictines, St. Benedict instructs young monks about how they are to listen to the instructions of their master. He counsels them: "Listen carefully . . . and attend . . . with the ear of your heart" (RB, Prologue 1). Listening with the "ear of the heart" is without doubt a different kind of listening. If the heart is at the core of our person and the seat of our capacity to receive and give love, then this kind of listening attends primarily not to ideas and their logic, but to relationships and love. If God is love (1 John 4:8), in love with us, is this not how we should listen to God?

How can we go about doing that kind of listening? A first step is to attend to the readings in order to listen for the words and phrases that truly speak to our hearts. What words and phrases speak to us about our relationship to God and to one another? What words do we feel called to cherish? What words of love do we hear? What do these words ask us to do? This kind of hearing (or reading) of the Scriptures is the first step in what our long-standing tradition of spirituality calls *lectio divina* ("divine reading").[4]

---

[3] Bernardin, *Guide for the Assembly*, 37.
[4] This would also serve Catholics who are increasingly adopting the practice of reading and praying the assigned readings before Sunday.

The second step follows. Mary sets us an example. Like her, we need to "treasure all these things in our heart" (Luke 2:51, paraphrased). We need to ponder and savor these words in the silence of our hearts. That is the second step of *lectio divina*. Part of that pondering is to let God's message of unconditional and all-embracing love seep into our being and to ask ourselves what that means for how we live our lives. Listening with the "ear of the heart" to what the readings say thrives only in an inner silence. "Liturgical silence is not merely an absence of words, a pause, or an interlude. Rather, it is a stillness, a quieting of spirits, a taking time and leisure to hear, assimilate, and respond."[5]

But does the typical celebration of the Liturgy of the Word allow time for that? To give us time for such reflection, GIRM 56 recommends that we observe appropriate brief periods of silence before the readings begin, after the first and second readings, and after the homily following the Gospel, for "by means of these, under the action of the Holy Spirit, the Word of God may be grasped by the heart and a response through prayer may be prepared." Silence gives time for the Spirit to work in us, for the Word to gestate and be born.[6] It is that Spirit, Jesus said to his disciples at his leave-taking, who will "teach you everything, and remind you of all that I have said to you" (John 14:26). Respecting these times of silence in the liturgy and helping people understand their purpose is a pastoral necessity.

Responding

Listening in silence with the "ear of the heart" opens us to accepting and acting on what is said, in loving obedience to God's word. The word "obey" derives from an intensified form of the Latin verb for listening; it comes from two Latin roots: *ob* + *audire*. That means not just to listen, but to listen carefully and thoroughly to what is said, all the way through to the end, in order to act on what it demands. That is what listening with the "ear of the heart" is about. It cannot help but lead to *responding* in love for God and for all and everything loved by God.

One more comment about Bernardin's idea of learning through proclamation of the Scripture readings to "be good listeners to one another,

---

[5] Bishops' Committee on the Liturgy, *Introduction to the Order of Mass: A Pastoral Resource of the Bishops' Committee on the Liturgy* (Washington, DC: USCCB, 2003), 32, no. 48.

[6] See text #4, "This is the Word of the Lord," by Ronald DeHondt, below.

to the Lord, to the world with all its needs." Medieval theologians spoke of three books of revelation: Scriptures, human experience throughout the course of history, and the world of nature. God speaks through all of them. Attending to that first book of revelation on Sunday can prepare and inspire us to listen more carefully to the other two books during the week. The art of listening learned on Sunday is to be used on weekdays as well. But it is not always easy to hear God's voice amid the din of daily life. We need to be on the alert for it and to make our own the attitude portrayed again and again in the Bible when God calls someone: "Here I am," and we need to cultivate the eager readiness of the young Samuel: "Speak, for your servant is listening" (1 Sam 3:10). We need to listen especially to hear God's voice in the cry of those who are poor and oppressed. God is particularly attentive to their cry, just as we must learn to be. They have much to teach us about God and Jesus' way of discipleship. Their cry is often a silent cry. The din around us and our responsibilities and preoccupations often drown it out. Their cry might be no more than that tiny whispering sound that Elijah heard outside his cave (1 Kgs 19:12). But if we are schooled in listening to God's voice in the proclamation of the Scripture readings, we can then learn to listen for it in daily life. That, in turn, can prepare us to return to the assembly with better listening skills and to listen more attentively to what God says to us in the Scriptures. The cycle between liturgy and life spirals on.

Gospel

"The reading of the Gospel constitutes the high point of the Liturgy of the Word" (GIRM 60). We cherish it because, as Peter professed, we believe that the Lord speaks to us in it: "Lord, to whom can we go? You have the words of eternal life" (John 6:68). That belief is shown in the words and rituals that surround the proclamation of the Gospel. Think for a moment of the care and ritual actions that surround the proclamation of the Gospel. The book itself is often beautifully crafted and artistically adorned and illustrated. During the entrance rites it has been carried in and placed on the altar. It is now carried aloft from the altar to the ambo in a mini-procession, often accompanied by candles. The Alleluia we sing acclaims Christ, whose word it is. The same greeting that began the Mass once again welcomes him into our midst: "The Lord be with you." After the Gospel passage is announced, we all sign ourselves on the forehead, lips, and heart and once more acclaim: "Glory to you, O Lord." A good question to ask participants is what do those actions mean? On more solemn feasts the book may also be incensed as a mark of honor. We stand to listen to the Gospel as a sign of great reverence. And when the Gospel has been proclaimed, Christ is again acclaimed: "Praise to you, Lord Jesus Christ." These marks of honor all attest to our faith that Christ himself is present and speaking to us when the Scriptures are proclaimed in the assembly (SC 7).

But what is the Gospel saying to us, what story does the Gospel tell? In answer to that question, people answer without hesitation that it tells the story of the life of Jesus, his words and deeds, his death and resurrection. That is the common narrative pattern, the story line, of all the Gospels from his baptism in the Jordan to his death on Calvary. But the Gospel tells not just the story of Jesus. His life story points the way for us. At the Last Supper he told his disciples that they know the way to his Father's house where he would go to prepare a place for them. When Thomas insisted that they did not know the way, Jesus answered, "I am the way" (John 14:6). He is the pioneer, the pathfinder of faith, and the one who has brought it to completion (Heb 12:2). That is the path his disciples are to follow.

So what *other story* does the Gospel tell? The Gospel tells the story we espouse as our own, our collective master story. In telling us the story of Jesus' life, it tells the story we are called to live out—to follow in his footsteps and to lose our lives in loving service to others "for my sake and the sake of the gospel" (Mark 8:35). The Book of the Gospels carried in solemn entrance procession and once again held high for its proclamation tells our story too. A poetic reflection by Gabe Huck sums it up this way: "Here's the kernel of ourselves . . . this book that dances now in incense sweet and sweet its alphabet to kiss."[7] This "kernel of ourselves," of our daily lives, has been brought with us into the assembly as we entered. Our lives are now named fully in the proclamation of the Gospel; they will be brought to the altar table with the bread and wine and offered to God during the Eucharistic Prayer.

The homily then breaks open the readings so that people can find the story of their lives told in the story of Jesus and understand how they are to enflesh that story in their own lives. At the beginning of his public ministry, Jesus captured the essence and aim of every homily. After reading

---

[7] Gabe Huck, "Book," LGWO, 45; text #7 below.

the Scriptures in his hometown synagogue at Nazareth, he said: "Today this scripture has been fulfilled in your hearing" (Luke 4:21). Creed and prayers of the faithful then bring the Liturgy of the Word to its conclusion.

Ambo and Altar

One other detail merits a final reflection. The GIRM notes the following: "It is a praiseworthy practice . . . to place the *Book of the Gospels* on the altar" in the entrance rites (173, 195). Why is that so? Is the altar no more than a convenient shelf on which to place the Book of the Gospels? If not, what connection is there between the Gospel and the altar? Christ is the connection. He speaks when the Scriptures are proclaimed (SC 7), and the rite of *Dedication of the Altar* notes that "Christian writers see in the altar a sign of Christ himself—hence they affirm: 'The altar is Christ.'"[8] Vatican II insists that the Liturgy of the Word and the Liturgy of the Eucharist "are so closely connected with each other that they form but one single act of worship" (SC 56). Using the image of food shared at table, the *General Introduction to the Lectionary for Mass* affirms this unbroken unity between Word and Eucharist when it writes: "The Church is nourished spiritually at the twofold table of God's Word and of the Eucharist"[9] (GILM 10). That, incidentally, is also why the church asks that great pains be taken to develop a design that ensures "the harmonious and close relationship of the ambo with the altar" (GILM 32). One act of worship celebrated at two tables, contributing by word and sacrament to the spiritual nourishment of God's people. The Liturgy of the Word leads seamlessly to the Liturgy of the Eucharist that enacts what the Word has proclaimed. That will be the focus of the next three chapters.

In sum

"Initiation into the mystery of Christ" (CCC 1075) is the common goal of catechesis and liturgy. Reaching that goal requires us to know the story of Christ and to make it our own. The story line of his life has to become the story line of our lives too. Together as a community our lives are to portray the story of Christ, to be a "letter of Christ," Paul tells the Corinthians, a letter "to be known and read by all" (2 Cor 3:2–3). Or in

---

[8] "Dedication of an Altar" 4, in *Dedication of a Church and an Altar*.

[9] Food is a common biblical image for the Word of God.

another image, together as a community we are called to be the face of Christ in our world. A long Eastern tradition among icon-writers holds that the face of every saint depicted in an icon together with Christ must show a family resemblance to his face.[10] Like individual tesserae, small colored stones that make up the mosaic, each of us is to be a small bit of color reflecting some aspect of Christ's face. Coming to know and imitate some detail of the image and life of Christ requires familiarity with the larger biblical story of his people and how he encapsulates it. That in turn demands that we relearn the art of listening in a noisy, deafening world. Indeed, that we relearn the art of "listening with the heart." It also calls us to ponder in the depths of our heart the story of God's love shown in Jesus and to discern what of that we can reflect in our lives.

The Mystagogy

Setting the stage

The environment for this session might well feature the Book of the Gospels, opened, enshrined, and flanked by candles. Inviting participants to approach and venerate the Book of the Gospels by touch, bow, or signing it, or signing our forehead, lips, and heart as at the Gospel would be fitting as part of the opening prayer. It could also be done, either when appropriate during the session, or at the conclusion of the reflective walk-through. Alternately, the Book of the Gospels might be brought in in procession and/or brought around for participants to touch, as happens with the scroll of the Torah in Jewish liturgy.

Table 4A

Topic slide for PowerPoint	
Title	Proclaiming, Listening, Responding to the Word
Visual	Book of the Gospels elevated by presider/deacon

[10] The practice of creating icons is commonly known as "writing" and the artists who do so are often described as "writers." This linguistic curiosity stems from a literal translation of the Greek term "iconography," in which *graphē* is typically understood as "writing." Some, however, have argued that this is a poor translation practice, and that "painting" and "painters" should be used instead.

Attending to experience

- *What do we do as part of the Liturgy of the Word? Who does what and where?*

Table 4B

Elicit the elements in detail

- *In a moment of silence, imagine and relive those things in memory.*
- *Name aloud the elements you love the most.*
- *What helps you most to listen to the readings and take them to heart?*

Reflections on the ritual actions and symbols

Shape of the rite

- *How do the parts of the Liturgy of the Word fit together? How are they related?*
- *In what ways is it like or unlike ordinary human conversation?*
- *How do we know that God speaks to us in the readings?*
- *What do the ritual dialogues before and after the readings tell us?*
- *What is the high point for you in the Liturgy of the Word?*

Table 4C

Themes	comparison to human conversation[11] dialogue / conversation address: God's word—ritual dialogue response: thanks be to God/creed/general intercessions
Title	Listening and responding
Visual	lector at ambo and assembly (local community)
Text #1	"Lord, to whom shall we go? You have the words of eternal life." (John 6:68)

Proclaiming

- *What is the meaning of the word "proclamation"?*
- *How is it different from other forms of speaking?*
- *What helps or hinders the proclamation for you?*

[11] The material in the tables is offered as a resource. The cells (rows) between darker lines in each table, here and hereafter, represent sample individual PowerPoint slides. The mystagogy can be conducted without the PowerPoint slides, using only the starter questions and live interaction, if the facilitator so wishes.

Table 4D

Themes	comparison to ordinary speech, declamation, etc.
Title	Proclaiming the Word
Visual	close-up of lector at ambo (local community)
Text #2	"Ambo" [read poem, insert lines: "like a rooftop" and "for proclaiming"]

Listening

- *What does it mean to "listen"?*
- *How is listening to the readings different from other kinds of listening?*
- *What helps or hinders listening to the readings?*
- *What are we to listen for in the readings?*
- *Why is there a period of silence after the readings?*

Table 4E

Themes	relearning the skill/art of listening listening for God's voice in our daily life in the world listening with the "ear of the heart" silence
Title	Learning to listen
Visual	assembly sitting in silence (local community)
Text #3	Guide for the Assembly [post and read text, underlining phrases:] "schooled in the art of listening" "good listeners" "to one another" "to the Lord" "to the world"
Title	Pondering in our hearts
Visual	Christ as teacher with open book (stained glass or icon)
Text #4	read poem: "This is the Word of the Lord"

Responding

- *What are our responses to the readings?*
- *Do the readings have any connections with daily living?*

• *What are the most compelling responses?*

Table 4F

Themes	receptive posture, ritual dialogue listening with "ear of the heart" creed, general intercessions
Title	Responding to the Word
Texts #5	"Speak, Lord, for your servant is listening." (1 Sam 3:10)
Visuals	assembly singing psalm response (local community) or Bible held to heart (close-up) or caring for someone who is sick

Gospel

• *What ritual dialogues and actions surround the Gospel?*
• *Why do we sign ourselves on the forehead, lips, and heart*
    at the beginning of the Gospel?
• *What do these actions and the dialogue tell us about the Gospel?*
• *Whose story does the Gospel tell?*
• *What stories does it tell about us?*

Table 4G

Themes	signs and words of reverence surrounding the Gospel Christ speaks in the Gospel (SC 7)
Title	A reading from the holy Gospel
Visual	deacon/presider elevating the Gospel Book
Text #6	"The Gospel of the Lord"/"Praise to you, Lord Jesus Christ"
Text #7	read "Book" [insert following phrase: "the kernel of ourselves"]
Title	Homily
Visual	image of Christ teaching (stained glass window)
Text #1	"Lord, to whom can we go? You have the words of eternal life." (John 6:68)
Text	"Today this scripture has been fulfilled in your hearing." (Luke 4: 21)

Ambo and Altar

- *Why is the Book of the Gospels placed on the altar?*
- *What is the liturgical relation between the ambo and the altar?*
- *How is that shown?*

Table 4H

Themes	two tables—word and sacrament altar sign of Christ who speaks in Gospel
Title	Two tables: ambo and altar
Visual	ambo and altar with harmonious design (local community's if true)
Text	"nourished at the twofold table of Word and Eucharist" (GILM 10)

Recap

Table 4I

Themes	witnessing the story and image of Christ to the world
Title	Proclaiming, listening, responding to the Word
Visuals	several images repeated from above
Text #1	"words of eternal life"

Texts

#1—John 6:68

"Lord, to whom shall we go? You have the words of eternal life."

#2—"Ambo," by Barbara Schmich (LGWO, 45)

Like a rooftop
a town square
a city set upon a hill,
this pulpit—lectern—ambo;
place of advantage
for proclaiming

> to the disadvantaged
> the good news of Christ.
>   (Barbara Schmich)

#3—Bernardin, *Guide for the Assembly,* 37

"Listening is a skill that grows dull in the barrage of words one hears all day long. Yet we have no substitute for it. In the liturgy we are schooled in the art of listening. What we do here, we are to do with our lives—be good listeners to one another, to the Lord, to the world with all its needs."
    (Bernardin, *Guide for the Assembly,* 37)

#4—"This is the Word of the Lord," by Ronald DeHondt
    (LGWO, 25)
"Silence
    as brief
    as the moment
    between
        Lord
        and
        Thanks
becomes the womb
    for Word proclaimed
    to begin
    the miracle
    of birth."
        (Ronald DeHondt)

#5—1 Sam 3:10
"Speak, for your servant is listening."

#6—Gospel acclamation (OM 16)
"The Gospel of the Lord."
"Praise to you, Lord Jesus Christ!"
    (*Roman Missal*)

#7—"Book," by Gabe Huck (LGWO, 45)
"The dance is rigid down the aisle,
a book embraced, held high, held dear:
the common carrier of the tales
on fiber come from cotton fields
and pulp from forest cut in Maine.
What earth has given hands have made
flat, thin and bound between two boards,
the pages covered now with marks
that image sounds that image all:
the pictures of pictures only
are letters gathered into words
and words lined up and bundled, tied—
yet here's the kernel of ourselves:
the poems, geneologies,
laws, letters, sayings, prophecies,
psalms, stories, visions handed on
from mouth to mouth and tongue to tongue
and page to page, a year or three
to tell it round again, this book
that dances now in incense sweet
and sweet it's alphabet to kiss."
(Gabe Huck)

Reflective Resources

Bernardin, Cardinal Joseph. *Guide for the Assembly*, 11–14. Chicago: Liturgy Training Publications, 1997.

Bernstein, Eleanor, ed. *Liturgical Gestures Words Objects*. Notre Dame, IN: Notre Dame Center for Pastoral Liturgy, 1995.

Connell, Martin. *Guide for the Revised Lectionary*. Chicago: Liturgy Training Publications, 1998.

Mahony, Cardinal Roger. *Gather Faithfully Together: Guide for Sunday Mass*, 27–20. Chicago: Liturgy Training Publications, 1997.

Mitchell, Nathan, ed. *Table Bread and Cup: Meditations on Eucharist*, 46–53. Notre Dame, IN: Notre Dame Center for Pastoral Liturgy, 2000.

Ramshaw, Gail. *Words around the Table*. Chicago: Liturgy Training Publications, 1991.

5

Presenting Gifts of Bread and Wine

Introduction

The presentation of the gifts is the first of three parts that make up the Liturgy of the Eucharist. The eucharistic prayer and the communion rite are the other two. The presentation of the gifts consists of the following ritual elements:

- preparation of the altar
- presentation of the gifts
- blessing prayer for the bread
- preparation of the cup
- blessing prayer for the cup
- invitation to prayer and response ("Pray brothers and sisters . . . / May the Lord accept. . .")
- prayer over the offerings

The mystagogy for this session will focus on the ritual action of presenting the bread and wine and the blessing prayers that may be said aloud for each of them.

Background Briefing

Shape and meaning of the Presentation

The Liturgy of the Eucharist begins with preparation of the altar. GIRM identifies several persons who can have a role to play. The deacon places the corporal, purificator, and vessels on the altar (94). Acolytes assist the deacon, and they prepare the altar themselves if there is no deacon (98, 190). And if there are no acolytes, laypersons can be deputed to carry out the preparation (100, 106). Preparation of the altar is like setting the dinner table in the sight of the guests. Done with choreographed grace and care, it heightens and focuses their attention on the importance and significance of the meal that is to come. The same is true for the Eucharist. Having community members other than the presider prepare the altar table already communicates silently that we gather at the table of the Lord as a priestly people who participate fully in the rite. This message is reinforced by how the gifts are presented.

GIRM 72 links the presentation of the gifts to what Jesus did at the Last Supper: "At the Presentation of the Gifts, bread and wine with water are brought to the altar, the same elements, that is to say, which Jesus took into his hands." On one level, the presentation is simply a practical action, bringing the bread and wine to the altar table. But does it have more meaning than that? GIRM 73 continues: "It is a praiseworthy practice for the bread and wine to be presented by the faithful. They are then accepted at an appropriate place by the Priest or the Deacon to be carried to the altar. Even though the faithful no longer bring from their own possessions the bread and wine intended for the liturgy as was once the case, nevertheless the rite of carrying up the offerings still keeps its spiritual efficacy and significance."

Several aspects of this statement are worth exploring for the meaning they can have for us. First, it is praiseworthy for the faithful to present the bread and wine. In many communities the presenters rotate from Sunday to Sunday, involving many members of the assembly over the course of time. We are a priestly people, called both by baptism and by the very nature of the liturgy to "full, conscious, and active participation" in the liturgical celebrations (SC 14). Carrying up the gifts, watching the procession, and accompanying it with song are all forms of participation.

Second, in ancient times the faithful brought bread and wine to the celebration. Early church writers indicate that this was expected of all. The bread and wine were deposited in a reserved place. Floor mosaics in the Catechumenal Hall in Aquileia (312–320 CE) depict people depositing loaves of bread in baskets and others bringing gifts in kind. Another mosaic shows the deacon carrying some of the bread forward at the presentation. He chose as much as was needed for the celebration, and the rest was distributed to those who were poor or in need.

Third, the gifts are brought up in a procession. A procession, as noted in chapter 3, is performed by "a representative few treading a representative distance: journey distilled." They march in our stead. In a nearby parish the procession with the gifts is led by processional cross and candles. As it moves up the aisle, people stand row by row, like the "wave" in a sports stadium. Standing up in this way is a sign that what is being presented is their gift.

Fourth, GIRM notes that people no longer bring bread and wine from home for the celebration. Since the early Middle Ages home-baked bread has been replaced by small unleavened hosts for a variety of reasons. For example, this extraordinary form of the communion breads gave graphic expression to the sense of awe and unworthiness prevalent in the piety of the time. Provision of the unleavened breads for communion was also left to "holy people," the members of religious communities, as a means of livelihood. That remains true today, but it is now increasingly left to church goods firms. This way of providing the hosts has removed one form of active participation in the presentation of the gifts by members of the local assembly. They no longer bring bread and wine from their homes in an informal procession that is a prelude to the formal procession with the gifts by a "representative few." Nevertheless, GIRM says, "the rite of carrying up the offerings still keeps its spiritual efficacy and significance." What, then, is this spiritual significance of our present practice? The meaning of the presentation of the gifts will now be explored at greater length with the help of the blessing prayers for the bread and wine.[1]

Presenting bread

The blessing prayer for the bread gives us some important clues about the spiritual significance of presenting this gift. The prayer reads as follows.

> Blessed are you, Lord God of all creation,
> for through your goodness we have received
> the bread we offer you:
> fruit of the earth and work of human hands,
> it will become for us the bread of life.
> R̰. Blessed be God for ever.[2]

---

[1] The individual phrases of these prayers can be shown on the visual presentation one by one, with matching images, as they are reflected on.

[2] *The Roman Missal, Third Typical Edition*, Order of Mass 23.

This blessing prayer identifies bread as a gift on several levels. The prayer says first of all that it is a *gift we have received from God*. But why should God, the Creator of this vast universe, be concerned with bread? Genesis tells the story of how God created the earth and all that is in it. Images of the universe taken by the Hubble space telescope capture the awesome immensity and beauty of what God has created. From that greatness and beauty, Scriptures say, we can come to know something of the even greater immensity and beauty of God (Wis 13:5; Rm 1:19–20). Yet this God of awe and majesty cares for the least of creatures. Genesis tells how God provides food for humans, and indeed for every bird and beast (Gen 1:29–30). God gives food to all living creatures (Ps 136:25). Bread is a gift we receive from God's lavish goodness.

The blessing prayer then says that bread is the *fruit of the earth*. Bread is so common in our lives that we seldom think about where it comes from. Bread is made of cereal grain, most commonly from wheat in our part of the world.[3] Cereal gains are the common source of starch in temperate zones and are forms of domesticated grass that sprout up from the earth. Their seeds, clustered in heads, are harvested and made into various forms of bread for everyday human consumption.

In simplest terms, the life cycle of wheat starts with the seeds being planted in the ground. When conditions of air and soil temperatures and soil moisture are favorable, the seeds begin to sprout roots, stems, and leaves. In so-called winter wheat, sown in the fall, the young plants become dormant during the winter and resume their growth in spring. They draw nutrients from rainfall and the soil to complete their growth. When the plants reach maturity in early or mid-summer, heads form and pollinated grains begin growing. A mature grain contains a small embryo and a larger supply of starch meant to feed the embryo for a new generation. When the mature grains are harvested and milled the starch forms the largest component in flour.

This biological process is truly amazing—how a tiny life-bearing embryo at the heart of the seed is able, with the help of simple nutrients and the proper conditions, to become a full-grown plant bearing numerous seeds ready to reproduce or to be made into bread. This cycle of life-death-life bears rich symbolic potential for human life as well. For the Christian, there is a cycle of birth-life-death-life hereafter.

---

[3] Other cereal grains include oats, rye, barley, millet, corn, rice.

Bread, our blessing prayer says, is also the *work of human hands*. We are all aware that farmers and bakers have had a hand in it. But stop and think. There is much more to it than that. The farmers who plant and harvest the wheat need farm machinery. That machinery requires people who make it, factories, manufacturing equipment, offices, computers, furniture. These, in turn, are the products of other workers and their equipment. When harvested, the wheat has to be transported by trucks and trains to mills, the milled flour to bakeries, and the bread to grocery stores where grocers price it and place it on shelves to be rung up by the cashier at the checkout counter. At each stage along the way, buildings, equipment, supplies, and human workers are needed. The "work of human hands" ripples outward, on and on. Producing the simple item we call bread indeed requires the work of so many hands.

Let's stay on this human level for a moment. Bread is what anthropologists call a condensed symbol. What is condensed in bread is the God-given nourishing potential of our earth and all the human work that has gone into its production. Bread bears the imprint of all that human work. It also bears the imprint of our use of bread day after day. Bread is a human product made for human consumption; it is made to be eaten. On a purely physiological level, bread nourishes our body, our bodily life. Bread that is shared nourishes us on another level. Because we feed on the same loaf of bread, it forges human bonds between those at table. We share not just physical nourishment but also our relationships and life together. We are a company—*com-pane*, bread-sharers. Like the grain of wheat, this sharing of bread also involves a dying to self and rising anew to a life together.

In a real sense, then, what is carried in procession to the altar table is not just the physical reality of bread. Rather, the bread is the symbol of all our work, our relationships, our lives, ourselves, our world. Condensed in that bread, these are all borne along in the procession to the altar. Should not all of us in the assembly walk in spirit with those "representative few" marching that "representative distance," to present our work, our lives, ourselves, our world for the offering still to come?

The blessing prayer names yet one more level of gift. The bread will become for us *the bread of life*. This bread placed on the altar table is destined to be further transformed into a saving gift for us, the bread of life. That is the culmination of a long process in which bread has been transformed and ultimately takes on religious and spiritual meaning.

That further transformation of the meaning of bread is not something we can accomplish. It is God's doing. Bread became the sign of God's special care and concern for the people of the covenant. In the story of the exodus (Gen 12), God instructed Moses that the people should eat roasted lamb and unleavened bread on the night before their departure from Egypt. Ever after they were to observe this ritual annually as the memorial of their deliverance.[4] During the exodus God fed them manna, an unknown "bread from heaven" (Exod 16:9–15), and brought them into a land of their own, a "land of wheat and barley" where they could "eat bread without scarcity" (Deut 8:8-9). To Israel God promised the gift of finest wheat (Ps 81:16) and eventually a feast of rich food on the mountain of the Lord in the end time (Isa 25:6). The prayer said at the breaking and sharing of bread at the beginning of their daily meals, and of unleavened bread (*matzah*) at the Passover Seder, reminded the Jews that bread is a symbol of God's covenant with them. By sharing the bread they affirm the covenant.

Shaped within that tradition, Jesus adapted and transformed the food language of his people. He broke bread, the opening ritual of all Jewish meals. He did it, however, with outcasts and sinners who at that time were considered unfit table companions. Such table-sharing amounted to a proclamation that God's reign is open to all, a scandal to the religious establishment of his day (Luke 15:1–2).[5] The image of a banquet became a parable for that same open invitation to feast in the reign of God (e.g., Matt 22:1–11). Jesus' bread of life discourse (John 6:25–59) takes up the story of manna in the desert and reinterprets the meaning of the "bread from heaven." God sent the Lord Jesus among us to be the true and living bread from heaven, so that those who eat of it might live forever: "This is the bread that comes down from heaven. . . . Whoever eats of this bread will live forever; and the bread that I will give for the life of the world is my flesh" (John 6:50–51).[6] In John's Gospel the last

---

[4] The Passover integrated two predecessor springtime religious rites celebrated with lamb and unleavened bread, that petitioned the gods for the fertility of the flock and fields. This is an example of the transformation of human and religious rituals into rituals of remembrance referred to in CCC 1145 and 1189.

[5] These verses form the lead-in to three parables of a God who rejoices over the finding of a lost sheep, a lost coin, and a lost son.

[6] John's account of the Last Supper has no words of institution. Incidentally, the word "lord" is derived from the Old English *hlaford*, a combination of two words: *hlaf*, from

part of that quotation is seen by scholars as the equivalent of Jesus' words at the Last Supper: "This is my body, which is given for you" (Luke 22:19). In giving himself over to death, Jesus became bread for the life of the world. Earlier he had said: "Very truly, I tell you, unless a grain of wheat falls into the earth and dies, it remains just a single grain; but if it dies, it bears much fruit" (John 12:24). The image of the death of the grain of wheat named the price he would pay to become bread for the life of the world. It would also be the price of the gift of self his followers would be asked to pay (John 12:25).

One further reflection can be added. Liturgists often wish that we could again use "real" loaves of leavened bread for the Eucharist, as was the case in the first centuries of the church. Such bread would more fully draw on the symbolic meaning of bread to be broken and shared than does the small individual wafers we now use. Cardinal Bernardin, however, sees a mystagogical potential that can be rescued in our present practice. He writes: "The unleavened bread is obviously not our usual bread but a simple bread, a bread of the poor. In this bread we cast our lot with the poor, knowing ourselves—however materially affluent—to be poor people, needy, hungry. Unless we acknowledge our hunger, we have no place at this table. How else can God feed us?"[7]

One might also see another symbolic meaning in this "simple bread." On a human level, such a small host, almost unsubstantial, seems totally inadequate to satiate human hunger. We need to be fed again and again. This suggests that we might also see the Eucharist as a holy meal that we need to celebrate again and again as we journey from our First Communion to our Last Communion, traditionally called *Viaticum*, that means "food for the journey" beyond life into eternity. But Eucharist received again and again during life might also be seen as "food for the journey," food with which we need to be fed along the path of Christian life on earth from initiation to death. Eucharist is what Gordon Lathrop has called a "hungry feast," an idea to which we return again.[8]

---

which we get the word "loaf," and *ord*, that means the "one who guards," or perhaps "brings," the loaf. We have lost the original meaning of such an apt English way to name Jesus as the one who feeds us.

[7] Cardinal Bernardin, *Guide for the Assembly*, 54.

[8] Gordon W. Lathrop, "The Hungry Feast," *Lutheran Forum* 11 (American Lutheran Publicity Bureau, 1977).

Presenting wine

The second gift presented at the altar table is wine. What is its spiritual significance? The blessing prayer for the wine offers us clues.

> Blessed are you, Lord God of all creation,
> for through your goodness we have received
> the wine we offer you:
> fruit of the vine and work of human hands,
> it will become our spiritual drink.
>   R/. Blessed be God for ever.[9]

Again, why should God, the Creator of this vast universe—immense space and uncounted galaxies beyond our comprehension—be concerned with so minor a thing as grapevines and wine? But God was concerned. Psalm 104:14–15 sings praise for God, who made everything.

> You cause the grass to grow for the cattle,
>   and plants for people to use,
> to bring forth food from the earth,
>   and wine to gladden the human heart

Like bread, wine is also a gift for our use that *we have received through God's goodness* and providence.

The blessing prayer calls wine the *fruit of the vine*. This way of naming wine is familiar to us from the accounts of the Last Supper (e.g., Matt 26:29). This phrase connects the wine to grapevines. Grapevines have roots, trunk, and branches. They are perennials with an annual life-cycle. At the end of one season, buds have formed that go dormant over the winter. Pruned in early spring, they awaken to life when the temperature is right. With the help of nutrients and water drawn from the ground and of the photosynthesis of sunlight, they send forth shoots that produce tendrils, stems with leaves, and stems with flower buds. After pollination, berries develop and ripen and become ready for harvest in the fall. Dormancy again sets in, preparing the grapevine for the next cycle. The wine that will be produced after the harvest is truly the gift of the vine and of the earth.

Wine, the blessing prayer says, is the *work of human hands*. Like bread, it involves the labor of many people—those who grow and prune the

---

[9] *The Roman Missal, Third Typical Edition*, Order of Mass 25.

vines; those who harvest the grapes; those who transport the grapes to the wineries; those who press the grapes to yield their juice, add yeast (and sugar in some cases) to set the process of fermentation underway; and those who bottle the wine and supervise its aging; those who transport the finished wine to retail stores, where it is priced, shelved, and rung up by the clerk at the checkout counter. For each of these activities, appropriate buildings, equipment, and other resources are required. These in turn also require other materials and workers. As with bread, wine is a condensed symbol bearing the imprint of many hands, workers' lives, and the world itself. All this is brought to the altar table at the presentation and set apart to be offered later as gift. Put another way, presenting the wine dedicates it for the act of offering that is to follow later in the Mass.

Through the work of human hands, this gift of God and mother earth has been transformed with newness of meaning. In its physical reality, wine is a drink that slakes human thirst. But it is more than that. It gladdens our hearts, the psalmist says. Like all fermented drinks, that take a long time and much effort to produce, it is often reserved for special occasions. On such occasions wine is commonly shared with others, and it is first offered as a toast to guests before it is consumed. Wine speaks of friendship, feast, and gladness; its transformed meaning is no longer simply slaking thirst.

The wine we bring to the altar table will be transformed yet again and take on additional new levels of symbolism. The blessing prayer says *it will become our spiritual drink*. What might that mean? The Bible presents us with a cluster of such meanings. Vine and vineyard are used by prophets and psalmist as a common image for Israel as the people of God and for God as the vineyard owner and vinedresser.

> You brought this vine out of Egypt,
>   you drove out the nations and planted it.
> You cleared the ground for it;
>   it took deep root and filled the land. (Ps 80:8–9)

> A pleasant vineyard, sing about it!
>   I, the Lord, am its keeper;
>   every moment I water it.
> I guard it night and day
>   so that no one can harm it. (Isa 27:2–3)[10]

---

[10] See also Ps 80:8–16.

This image of the vineyard lies behind some of Jesus' parables (e.g., Mark 12:1–12). More importantly, he identified himself as the vine, of which his disciples are the branches (John 15:1–5). It is from the living vine and by abiding in it that they draw the power to bear fruit.

A second strand in that biblical cluster of symbolic meanings is eschatological.

> On this mountain the Lord of hosts will make for all peoples
> a feast of rich food, a feast of well-aged wines,
> of rich food filled with marrow, of well-aged wines strained
> clear. (Isa 25:6)

At the Last Supper Jesus also used that eschatological image: "Truly I tell you, I will never again drink of the fruit of the vine until that day when I drink it new in the kingdom of God" (Mark 14:25; Matt 26:24; Luke 22:18).[11]

A third strand of symbolic meaning is also found in Scripture. Wine is the "blood of grapes," used both as drink (Deut 32:14; Sir 39:26) and as libation (Sir 50:15). This connection with blood may well have been suggested to the Israelites by the color of red wine. Blood, in their understanding, is where the life-giving breath of God resides. The creation account says: "then the Lord God formed man from the dust of the ground, and breathed into his nostrils the breath of life; and the man became a living being" (Gen 2:7). It is the breath of God that gives life and is the life force within humans and animals. For that reason, kosher regulations forbad human consumption of blood (Gen 9:4). Life-bearing blood took on a number of meanings: sacrificial libations (Lev 4:5–7), purification and atonement (Heb 9:22), and covenantal bonds between those who share it. A prime example of a covenant sealed by blood is found in Exodus 24:3–8. Oxen were sacrificed, and Moses dashed half of the collected blood on the altar representing God and half on the people with the words, "the blood of the covenant." In the institution accounts of Mark and Matthew, this formula is quoted literally in Jesus' words over the cup of wine (Mark 14:24; Matt 26:28). His words that the wine in the cup is his "blood of the covenant" mean that it is his life, himself, that will be poured out for the many, for the forgiveness

---

[11] Some scholars note that these eschatological words in Luke precede the account of the institution, implying that it is already within the kingdom that the supper takes place.

of sins. Elsewhere he spoke of his death as the "cup that the Father has given me" to drink (John 18:11). As with bread, wine aptly serves as a symbol for a dying to self that brings forth life. Like bread, wine is also a symbol of life given in death for the nourishment and happiness of another. A portion of a reflective poem by Mark Searle says it well.

> Food and drink are creatures which achieve fulfillment
> in being put at the disposal of others:
> they exist to serve the needs of others;
> their destiny is met in their destruction.[12]

This biblical cluster of symbols names the spiritual meaning the wine will take on as the eucharistic celebration continues. The wine now brought forward is to be transformed into the sacrament of Christ's gift of himself poured out for our salvation.

We should also note the symbolic use of wine at Jewish and Christian meals. The Jewish prayer after meals has traditionally been said over a glass of wine, technically called the "cup of blessing" at the Seder. The prayer over this cup thanks God for the land and all the blessings of the covenant. "You shall eat your fill and bless the LORD your God for the good land he has given you" (Deut 8:10). In the eucharistic meal of Christians, we also use the prayer over the cup of wine to remember the covenant sealed in Jesus' death: "This cup that is poured out for you is the new covenant in my blood" (Luke 22:20). This remembrance is more than mere recollection. It inserts us into the covenantal action of Jesus. "The cup of blessing that we bless, is it not a sharing in the blood of Christ?" (1 Cor 10:16).

Dialogue of the gift I

One more reflection will serve as a summary of this briefing and further set the presentation of bread and wine into a rich perspective.

In the presentation of the gifts, bread and wine are identified as gifts of God, gifts of the earth, and gifts of human labor—gifts that are destined to become our spiritual food and drink.[13] They are part of what E. C. Miller calls a "dialogue of the gift," that is really a "dialogue of

---

[12] Mark Searle, "Bread & Wine," LGWO, 53.

[13] This paragraph is taken, with slight modifications, from an article I have written for the *Dictionary of the Passion*, to be published in several languages by Città Nuova.

love."[14] Creation is God's act of gift-giving. It includes not only material creation and all living things, but also humanity's ability to actualize the world's potential and present it back to God as a gift, a gift also meant to be shared for the good of all. In presenting the bread and wine, Miller notes, the baptized formally declare their willingness to reenter into the dialogue of gift initiated in creation, a dialogue that had lapsed into silence in the fall. In our self-sufficiency and self-centeredness we had forgotten who has given us these gifts and that they are intended not for us alone but for the use of the entire human family. Bread and wine are ultimately God's gift. They are also the work of human hands. What is condensed in them is all the collaborative human labor that has gone into their production. That circle of human labor ripples out to include not only farmers, millers and bakers, grape growers and vintners, but a multitude of other hands that make their work possible. In effect, what we place on the table is all our work, our very lives, and creation itself, as a gift to be offered to God in thanksgiving and to be used in the service of others. At Mass we are all meant to accompany the gift bearers in the spirit as they walk up the aisle, each carrying our self-gift in our hands to place it on the altar table. The prayer over the gifts for the Twentieth Sunday in Ordinary Time expresses well the dialogue of the gift that takes place within the rite of presentation.

> Receive our oblation, O Lord,
> by which is brought about a glorious exchange,
> that, by offering what you have given,
> we may merit to receive your very self.

It is fitting that we place this gift of ourselves on the altar table. The altar table is the reflection of ourselves, who are "spiritual altars on which the sacrifice of a holy life is offered to God" (*Rite of Dedication of an Altar* 2).

A final series of questions: How can we celebrate the presentation of the gifts in such a way that it constantly provides us a rich experience waiting to be broken open in mystagogy? How can that mystagogy help us understand and make our own the lifelong journey of self-giving in imitation of and in union with Christ's self-giving for which this rite prepares us? The next chapter will help us name that.

---

[14] E. C. Miller, "Presentation of Gifts: Orthodox Insights for Western Liturgical Renewal," *Worship* 60 (1986): 22–38, quoting Dumitru Staniloae.

The Mystagogy

Setting the stage

The environment for this session could feature an artistic arrangement of a loaf of bread and a carafe of red wine on a small table covered with swatches of cloth. In addition, candles or flowers might also be part of the arrangement.

Table 5A

Topic slide for PowerPoint[15]	
Title	Presenting Gifts of Bread and Wine
Visual	Procession with gifts (local community)

Attending to experience

- *What happens at the presentation of the gifts?*

Table 5B

Elicit the elements in detail

- *In a moment of silence, remember and relive that ritual presentation.*
- *Name aloud the elements of the presentation you love the most.*
- *Which elements help you best to enter into what the presentation means?*

Shape of the Presentation

- *How would the meaning of the presentation be different if we all brought bread and wine, as people did in the early church?*

Table 5C

Themes	early church practice, bread and wine from home how we participate in procession walking in spirit with the "representative few"
Title	Presenting Bread and Wine
Visuals	Catechumenal Hall (Aquilea), floor mosaic panels showing people putting bread in baskets, deacon carrying loaves hung from pole on shoulder or similar images (if above not available)

[15] The material in the tables is offered as a resource. The cells (rows) between darker lines in each table, here and hereafter, represent sample individual PowerPoint slides. The mystagogy can be conducted without the PowerPoint slides, using only the starter questions and live interaction, if the facilitator so wishes.

Title	Procession with the Gifts
Visual	procession with the gifts (local community)
Text #1	GIRM 23 entire text, underline "spiritual significance and efficacy"
Title	What is the Spiritual Significance?
Text	clues from the prayers for the presentation

Reflection on the ritual actions and symbols

Bread

- *What does the blessing over bread say that bread is?*
- *What is bread?*

Table 5D

Themes	gift of the God of all creation, gift of the earth
Title	Blessing Prayer for the Bread
Text #2	"Blessed are you, Lord God of all Creation for through your goodness we have received the bread we offer you"
Visuals	stars and galaxies [Hubble], earth from space [then overlaid]
Text	bread: gift of God of majesty
Title	"fruit of the earth"
Visuals,	wheat fields, heads of wheat (close-up)
Text	gift of the earth

- *Who is involved in producing bread?*

Table 5E

Themes	gift of human work made for human consumption condensed symbol of much human work
Title	"work of human hands"
Visuals	workers harvesting wheat hands kneading/baking hands cutting loaf (close-up)
Text	gift of human labor

- *What purposes does bread serve?*
- *Why do we call it the "staff of life"?*

Table 5F

Themes	staple diet of bread nourishes bodily life sharing bread expresses human life together (family, friends)
Title	Shared
Visuals	hands breaking loaf (close-up) people sharing bread at table, or picnic

- *How is bread used symbolically in the Scriptures?*
- *How can we relate that deep meaning to the hosts we use?*

Table 5G

Themes	"will become the bread of life" manna in the desert—God's provident care breaking bread as reminder of covenant banquet image of the end-time (Isaiah) Jesus' inclusive meal practice parables of the kingdom "grain of wheat must die" "bread that I will give . . . for life of world" a simple bread, a hungry feast
Title	"the bread of life"
Visual	Last Supper
Text	"bread that I will give . . . for life of world" (John 6:51)
Visual	host
Text #3	"a simple bread, a bread of the poor. . . . Unless we acknowledge our hunger, we have no place at this table. How else can God feed us?" (Bernardin, *Guide for the Assembly*, 54)

Wine

- *What does the blessing over wine say that wine is?*

Table 5H

Themes	gift of the God of all creation, fruit of the vine
Title	Blessing Prayer for the Wine
Text #4	"Blessed are you, Lord God of all Creation for through your goodness we have received the wine we offer you"
Visuals	stars and galaxies [Hubble], earth from space [overlaid]
Text	wine: gift of God of majesty
Title	"fruit of the Vine"
Visuals	vineyard, clusters of grapes hanging on vine, goblet of red wine
Text	gift of the vine

- *What is wine?*
- *Who is involved in producing wine?*

Table 5I

Themes	gift of human work condensed symbol of much human work made for human consumption, for feast
Title	"work of human hands"
Visuals	worker pruning vines worker picking grapes baskets of grapes vintner and wine kegs
Text	gift of human labor

- *What purposes does wine serve?*
- *Why do we reserve it for special occasions?*
- *Why do we use wine for toasts?*

Table 5J

Themes	wine slakes thirst sharing wine shared gladness, feast (family, friends) toasts to honor guests
Title	Shared
Visuals	carafe and goblet of wine (close-up) sharing toast at table

• *How is wine used symbolically in the Scriptures?*

Table 5K

Themes	"will become our spiritual drink" Israel God's vineyard, vine well-aged wines at the end-time banquet (Isaiah) Jesus' parables of the vine and branches "the cup that I must drink" "the new covenant in my blood"
Title	"our spiritual drink"
Visuals	goblet of wine ["cup of blessing"] Last Supper
Text	"This cup is the new covenant in my blood." (2 Cor 11:25)

Dialogue of the Gift

• *What gifts do we place on the altar table at the presentation?*
• *What is the meaning of that?*
• *Who gives us the gifts we bring?*
• *What gift do we hope to receive in return?*

Table 5L

Themes	the ancient Christian language of the "holy/marvelous exchange" God's gift of creation, life, incarnate Son, eternal life our gift of thanks, self in service of God's reign
Title	The Spiritual Significance?
Text	bread and wine to be transformed into spiritual food and drink
Text	in a dialogue of gift
Text #5	Prayer over the Gifts, Twentieth Sunday in Ordinary Time [insert entire text, underline following] " glorious exchange"

Recap

Table 5M

Themes	summary of above themes
Title	Presenting Gifts of Bread and Wine
Visual	procession with gifts
Text	bringing the gift of our lives
Text	a holy exchange of gifts
Text #6	"Pray . . . that my sacrifice and yours may be acceptable to God. . . ." "May the Lord accept the sacrifice. . . ."

Texts

#1—GIRM 73

"Even though the faithful no longer bring from their own possessions the bread and wine intended for the liturgy as was once the case, nevertheless the rite of carrying up the offerings still keeps its spiritual efficacy and significance."
(GIRM 73)

#2—Prayer of Blessing (OM 23)

"Blessed are you, Lord God of all creation,
for through your goodness we have received
the bread we offer you:
fruit of the earth and work of human hands,
it will become for us the bread of life.
    R⁷. Blessed be God for ever."
(*Roman Missal*)

#3—Bernardin, *Guide for the Assembly*, 54

"The unleavened bread is obviously not our usual bread but a simple bread, a bread of the poor. In this bread we cast our lot with the poor, knowing ourselves—however materially affluent—to be poor people, needy, hungry. Unless we acknowledge our hunger, we have no place at this table. How else can God feed us?"
(Bernardin, *Guide for the Assembly*, 54)

#4—Prayer of Blessing (OM 25)

"Blessed are you, Lord God of all creation,
for through your goodness we have received
the wine we offer you:
fruit of the vine and work of human hands,
it will become our spiritual drink.
    R̮. Blessed be God for ever."
(Roman Missal)

#5—Prayer over the Gifts, Twentieth Sunday in Ordinary Time (MR)

"Receive our oblation, O Lord,
by which is brought about a glorious exchange,
that, by offering what you have given,
we may merit to receive your very self."
    (Prayer over the Gifts, Twentieth Sunday in Ordinary Time)

#6—Orate (OM 29)

"Pray . . .
that my sacrifice and yours
may be acceptable to God, . . ."
"May the Lord accept the sacrifice."
(Roman Missal)

Reflective Resources

Bernardin, Cardinal Joseph. *Guide for the Assembly*, 15–16. Chicago: Liturgy Training Publications, 1997.

Bernstein, Eleanor, ed. *Liturgical Gestures Words Objects*. Notre Dame, IN: Notre Dame Center for Pastoral Liturgy, 1995.

Guardini, Romano. "Bread and Wine," cited in *How Firm a Foundation: Voices of the Early Liturgical Movement*, compiled and edited by Kathleen Hughes, 115–116. Chicago: Liturgy Training Publications, 1990.

Mahony, Cardinal Roger. *Gather Faithfully Together: Guide for Sunday Mass*, 20–25. Chicago: Liturgy Training Publications, 1997.

Ramshaw, Gail. *Words around the Table*. Chicago: Liturgy Training Publications, 1991.

Rech, Photina. *Wine and Bread*. Trans. by Heinz R. Kuehn. Chicago: Liturgy Training Publications, 1998.

6

Giving Thanks, Offering the Gift, and Interceding

Introduction

The eucharistic prayer is the second part of the Liturgy of the Eucharist. The prayer consists of the following parts:[1]

- opening dialogue
- thanksgiving (preface)
- holy, holy, holy acclamation (*sanctus*)
- thanksgiving continued (post-*sanctus*)
- invocation of the Spirit (consecratory *epiclesis*)
- institution account
- memorial acclamation
- remembrance (*anamnesis*)
- offering
- invocation of the Spirit (communion *epiclesis*)
- intercessions (for living and dead)
- concluding doxology
- great amen acclamation

[1] This list is adapted from GIRM 79. This pattern is common, though there are some variations in different eucharistic prayers.

The mystagogy for this session will touch lightly on several of these elements, but it will focus especially on the institution account, the *anamnesis*, and the offering.

Background Briefing

Structure and meaning

From the presentation of the gifts the liturgy moves to the second part of the Liturgy of the Eucharist, the eucharistic prayer. GIRM 78 describes the basic structure and meaning of the eucharistic prayer in these words:

> Now the center and high point of the entire celebration be-gins, namely, the Eucharistic Prayer itself, that is, the prayer of thanksgiving and sanctification. The Priest calls upon the people to lift up their hearts towards the Lord in prayer and thanks-giving; he associates the people with himself in the Prayer that he addresses in the name of the entire community to God the Father through Jesus Christ in the Holy Spirit. Furthermore, the meaning of this Prayer is that the whole congregation of the faithful joins with Christ in confessing the great deeds of God and in the offering of Sacrifice.

The meaning of the eucharistic prayer is captured in those last two phrases: "confessing the great deeds of God" and "offering the Sacrifice." These are the themes of the two major parts of the prayer. Several preliminary comments on GIRM 78 are in order before we take up those two major parts.

Whose prayer is it?

The presider is to "associate the people with himself." The preface dialogue between presider and people establishes that the prayer to follow is the prayer of the entire assembly, presider and people. Though proclaimed by the presider, the prayer is cast in the first person plural. It is ours. The *Catechism of the Catholic Church* puts it very clearly: "In the celebration of the sacraments, the whole assembly is *leitourgos* [lit-urgist], each member according to his own function, but in the 'unity of the Spirit' who acts in all" (CCC 1144, also 1188).

We should not take our role as *leitourgos* too exclusively. After the opening greeting and response, the preface dialogue (OM 33) continues:

℣. Lift up your hearts.
℟. We lift them up to the Lord.
℣. Let us give thanks to the Lord our God.
℟. It is right and just.

This is not just a polite liturgical admonition to pay attention, like schoolchildren. It literally reminds us to lift up our hearts to where the Risen Savior presides as the "minister [*leitourgos*] in the sanctuary and the true tent that the Lord, and not any mortal, has set up" (Heb 8:2). The dialogue invites us to join that eternal heavenly liturgy, where the Risen Lord "always lives to make intercession" (Heb 7:25). It is that heavenly liturgy that we celebrate on earth under the presidency of Christ, our *leitourgos*, whose presence in the assembly is veiled in sign and symbol—the gathered assembly, word, presider, and bread and wine (SC 7).

How is it enacted?

How is participation in the eucharistic prayer enacted? The president's role is identified not only by proclaiming the prayer aloud but also by standing posture, vesture, and arms upraised in the ancient gesture of the *orans*. Of the assembly's role, GIRM 78 notes: "The Eucharistic Prayer requires that everybody listens to it with reverence and in silence." Listening with the "ear of the heart," described earlier, would be an appropriate way to think of this silence. But reverent silence is not the only way the assembly's participation is expressed. Kneeling after the Holy, Holy, Holy until the great amen is another expression.[2]

GIRM 34 had earlier called attention to another, more primary form of participation for the Mass as a whole: "Since the celebration of Mass by its nature has a 'communitarian' character, both the dialogues between the Priest and the assembled faithful, and the acclamations are of great significance, for they are not simply outward signs of communal celebration but foster and bring about communion between Priest and

---

[2] The official version of GIRM issued by Rome had allowed standing from the preface dialogue through the doxology, but left the final decision to the episcopal conferences. The USCCB decided to keep the kneeling posture (GIRM 43) that has been traditional in this country.

people." This is explained further in the following paragraph, GIRM 35: "The acclamations and the responses of the faithful to the Priest's greetings and prayers constitute that level of participation that is to be made by the assembled faithful in every form of the Mass, so that the action of the whole community may be clearly expressed and fostered."

The opening dialogue with the presider, the interspersed acclamations, and the great amen that ratifies all that has been proclaimed, are significant verbal forms of participation by the faithful, along with their reverent silence and kneeling posture. We turn now to the two major sections of the eucharistic prayer.

Giving thanks

To what does the assembly say the great amen? The first part of the eucharistic prayer is centered on remembrance and thanksgiving. It begins with the preface and continues through the institution account. It is an extended recital of what God has done for us in creation and salvation, culminating in the life, death, and resurrection of Jesus. After the consecratory *epiclesis*, that asks God to transform the bread and wine, this part of the prayer sums up the recital of God's saving deeds with the institution narrative. True to its Jewish heritage, Christian prayer is rooted first of all in remembering what God has done for us. The recital of God's great deeds in short prayers (e.g., the collects) can be as brief as a phrase or even an adjective joined to God's name in the address of the prayer ("Merciful God . . ."); it can be extended into a fulsome recital of significant moments in salvation history, as in the eucharistic prayer. In keeping with Jewish usage, the word "remember/remembrance" (*zkr/ zikaron*) means more than an act of mere recollection, merely going back in memory to a past event. It always carries with it a sense of our actual presence to the deeds being remembered (see, e.g., Deut 5:2–4). Such a remembrance of God's great deeds is meant to evoke an attitude of praise and thanks for salvation being received here and now. The eucharistic prayer can also be seen as a form of creed, calling us to confess faith in those great deeds, as GIRM 78 states.

Offering the gift and interceding

The second part of the eucharistic prayer focuses on offering the sacrifice and interceding. This second part of the prayer begins with words such as: "Therefore as we celebrate the memorial. . . ." This part of the prayer voices our response in several ways: offering ourselves as sacrifice with Christ, asking God to transform the assembly into the Body of Christ through the power of the Holy Spirit (communion *epiclesis*), and interceding for living and deceased members of the church and for the world. Transformed, we are to continue the work of Christ on earth.

The two parts of the eucharistic prayer are thus meant to evoke a dual response: thankful remembrance of God's saving deeds and intercession for God to continue those saving actions. Again, Christian prayer is faithful to the Jewish practice it has inherited. If what God has done is not locked in the past and God remains faithful, then surely God will continue to carry out that saving plan in the future. That is why we intercede with God to remember and to act. Remembrance and intercession are the two basic components of Jewish prayer inherited by the Christian community; we are a community of memory and hope.

Meaning for life

What does the eucharistic prayer mean for Christians? Several elements of this prayer are of great importance for a eucharistic spirituality that can flow out into daily life and shape it.[3] First, the words of institution end with the Lord's command: "Do this in remembrance of me" (Luke 22:19). This is more than a simple rubrical direction to repeat his supper actions of taking bread and wine, saying the blessing over them, breaking the bread, and giving the bread and wine to his disciples to eat and drink. Jesus gave new reality and meaning to the bread, naming it his "body given up for you," and to the wine, naming it his "blood poured out for you and for many."[4] The meaning of his

---

[3] The remaining paragraphs of this briefing are taken with further editing from my article, "A Mystagogy of the Eucharist," *Liturgical Ministry* 20 (Fall 2011): 163–164.

[4] A technical note: since the Middle Ages the recital of the words of Jesus in the institution narrative have been seen as the moment of consecration of the bread and wine. Christ's presence in the eucharistic species is acknowledged by the elevations and genuflections by the priest, the assembly's reverent silence, and the practice of ringing bells and incensing the species. Some strands of current theology see the entire eucharistic prayer as consecratory. This is based on a 2001 decree in which Rome recognized the validity of Mass celebrated with the ancient anaphora of Addai and Mari, that does not have an institution account. See Robert Taft, "Mass without Consecration?" *Worship* 77 (2003): 482–509.

entire life is thus summed up in the death to which he freely commits himself with these words. It is himself that he gives.[5] His life had been one of self-emptying service for the coming of God's reign, one of total self-giving in love (Phil 2:5–11). That same total giving of themselves in love is the "this" his followers are also to do ever after in memory of him.[6]

Second, the portion of the eucharistic prayer that follows the recital of Christ's command (technically called the *anamnesis*) is a pivotal moment in the response of the assembly, linking liturgy to life. In the implementation and catechesis of the Vatican II reform of the Mass this *anamnesis* paragraph has not received the pastoral and catechetical attention it rightly deserves. GIRM says that "in this very memorial, the Church—and in particular the Church here and now gathered—offers in the Holy Spirit the spotless Victim to the Father. The Church's intention, however, is that the faithful not only offer this spotless Victim but also learn to offer themselves . . ." (GIRM 79f, also SC 48). The text of Eucharistic Prayer III expresses this beautifully.

> Therefore, O Lord, as we celebrate the memorial
> of the saving Passion of your Son,
> his wondrous Resurrection
> and Ascension into heaven,
> and as we look forward to his second coming,
> we offer you in thanksgiving
> this holy and living sacrifice. (OM 113)

The phrase "living sacrifice" is New Testament language for Christian life (e.g., Rom 12:1). It is at this moment that all of us in the assembly complete what we began in the presentation of the gifts, when we presented bread and wine as the condensed symbols of our work, our lives, ourselves. We now offer the gift of daily witness and self-giving

---

[5] As noted in the previous chapter, in the Hebrew and Aramaic languages of that time, blood can have the meaning of the inner life-force in humans, since that is where the breath of God resides. The body is how that life-force expresses itself outwardly. Each term stands for the entire person, rather than for only one physical part.

[6] That same attitude of self-giving service is portrayed in John's Gospel, that recounts the washing of feet instead of the institution account. There Jesus gives this command: "So if I, your Lord and Teacher, have washed your feet, you also ought to wash one another's feet. For I have set you an example, that you also should do as I have done to you" (John 13:14–15).

service in the world, our very lives, as a "holy and living sacrifice" in union with the self-offering of Christ.[7]

This offering of ourselves in union with Christ is not always stated explicitly in the *anamnesis*, but it is often implied in what follows. Many eucharistic prayers go on to ask God to make of us a living sacrifice, or to accept us together with Christ. For example, in Eucharistic Prayer IV we pray that, "gathered into one body by the Holy Spirit, [we] may truly become a living sacrifice in Christ to the praise of your glory." In Eucharistic Prayer for Reconciliation II, we humbly beseech God "to accept us also, together with your Son."

We might note at this point that language of offering, giving, and gift abound in the eucharistic prayers. For example, in Eucharistic Prayer I we pray:

> we, your servants and your holy people,
> offer to your glorious majesty
> from the gifts that you have given us,
>
> . . .
>
> the holy Bread of eternal life
> and the Chalice of everlasting salvation. (OM 92)

And in Eucharistic Prayer III we ask:

> May he make of us
> an eternal offering to you. (OM 113)

Our hope is that these gifts, received and given, may finally be caught up in the heavenly liturgy, there to be offered eternally in the presence of God. So in Eucharistic Prayer I, we ask God to

> command that these gifts be borne
> by the hands of your holy angel
> to your altar on high . . . (OM 94)

In prayers such as these, the "dialogue of the gift" between God and us, that we explored earlier, continues. What we offered at the presentation

---

[7] Eucharistic Prayer I in *The Book of Common Prayer* has a striking prayer parallel to this: "And here we offer and present unto thee, O Lord, our selves, our souls and bodies, to be a reasonable, holy, and living sacrifice unto thee. . . ."

of the gifts was bread and wine, symbols of ourselves. It is now ourselves that we offer.

Offering ourselves, our lives, as an acceptable gift in union with Christ is something we would never have dared to imagine we can do. But that is exactly what Vatican II has taught. The Dogmatic Constitution on the Church (*Lumen Gentium*) states that

> all their works, prayers and apostolic endeavors, their ordinary married and family life, their daily occupations, their physical and mental relaxation, if carried out in the Spirit, and even the hardships of life, if patiently borne—all these become "spiritual sacrifices acceptable to God through Jesus Christ." Together with the offering of the Lord's body, they are most fittingly offered in the celebration of the Eucharist. And so, worshipping everywhere by these holy actions, the laity consecrate the world itself to God.[8]

This is why we have gathered, to offer with Christ our work, our lives, and our world. This is truly a pivotal moment in the celebration, one of great significance for connecting eucharist and daily life. We will return to this theme in the last chapter.

Third, the eucharistic prayer concludes with the great amen. It solemnly affirms this great prayer of giving thanks, offering the gift, and interceding. It also demands a commitment of us. Acclaiming it three times focuses our attention on a word said so often in the liturgy that we tend to ignore it. But it is truly a word that defines and sums up the entirety of the liturgy. We shall also reflect on this amen at greater length in the final chapter.

In sum

The eucharistic prayer is the center of the entire celebration. In it we remember with thanks and praise all the great deeds of God. In remembering those deeds, we encounter their saving effects once again. The recital of salvation history culminates in the narrative of the institution account. In that narrative, we hear Jesus' command to do with our lives what he did with his, to give ourselves in loving service for others. In

---

[8] Vatican II, *Lumen Gentium* 34. Online at www.vatican.va/archive/hist_councils /ii_vatican_council/documents/vat-ii_const_19641121_lumen-gentium_en.html.

the second part of the prayer, we offer ourselves to God in union with Christ as a "holy and living sacrifice," bringing to completion the initial presentation of ourselves with the bread and wine earlier placed on the altar table. We then ask God to continue the work of salvation, to transform us into the Body of Christ, interceding for the church living and deceased, and ready to be sent out on mission to the world at the conclusion of the celebration.

The Mystagogy

Setting the stage

The environment for this session could feature the *Roman Missal*, enshrined and flanked by candles. The *Missal* could be opened to the illustrated page at the beginning of the eucharistic prayers. Inviting participants to approach and view or touch the *Missal* would be fitting as part of the opening prayer. It could also be done either when appropriate during the session or at the conclusion of the reflective walk-through. Eucharistic Prayer III could also be proclaimed at the conclusion of the session.

Table 6A

Topic slide for PowerPoint[9]	
Title	Giving Thanks, Offering the Gift, Interceding
Visual	figure extending hands over gift in blessing, orans figure on side (Catacomb of St. Callistus, third century)[10]

Attending to experience

• *In a moment of silence, recall the words or phrases you remember from the eucharistic prayers.*

---

[9] The material in the tables is offered as a resource for facilitators who wish to use PowerPoint. The cells (rows) between darker lines in each table represent individual sample slides. The mystagogy can be conducted using only the starter questions and live interaction, if the facilitator so wishes.

[10] An image may be found online at en.wikipedia.org/wiki/Catacombs_of_Rome #mediaviewer/File:Eucharistic_bread.jpg.

- *Name aloud the words or phrases you love the most.*
- *Invite people to repeat that word or phrase and say why.*
- *What helps you best to enter into the eucharistic prayer?*
- *What attitudes or responses does the prayer invoke?*

Whose prayer?

- *Whose prayer is it?*
- *How is our participation in the eucharistic prayer shown; what forms does it take?*

Table 6B

Elicit the elements in detail: preface dialogue; use of plural; acclamations; amen	
Title	Joining the Liturgy above
Visual	Lamb on throne, surrounded by elders (heavenly liturgy)
Text #1	"Lift up your hearts." "We lift them up to the Lord."

Giving thanks

- *In the first part of the prayer, what do we remember?*

Table 6C

Themes	saving deeds of God culmination in paschal mystery
Title	Remembering and Thanking
Text #1	"Let us give thanks to the Lord our God." "It is right and just."
Visual	"Paschal Mystery" (Gisele Bauche attribution)
Text	for all that [sample layout of text beside the visual] God has done in creation and salvation, and especially in the life, death, resurrection of Jesus and the sending of the Spirit

- *What do Jesus' words in the Supper account mean?*

Table 6D

Themes	body, blood = self "do this" = give self "wash each other's feet" = give self in service
Title	"Do this in memory of me"
Text	"this is my body, given for you"
Text	"this is my blood, poured out for you"
Visuals	Giotto matched paintings: Last Supper and washing of feet
Text	two commands

Offering the gift and interceding

- *In the second part of the prayer, what do we offer? For what do we pray?*

Table 6E

Themes	offering a holy and living sacrifice offering of self and acceptance dialogue of gift
Title	Offering the Gift
Text #2	"Therefore, O Lord, as we celebrate the memorial of the saving Passion of your Son, . . . we offer you in thanksgiving this holy and living sacrifice." [underline "we offer you" and "this holy and living sacrifice"]
Text #3	"May he make of us an eternal offering to you" (Eucharistic Prayer III) [underline the last four words]
Title	**a Pivotal Moment!**
Text #4	GIRM 79f [insert entire text, then underline these phrases:] "offer this unblemished sacrificial Victim" "learn to offer their very selves" (GIRM 79f)
Title	offering the liturgy of life
Text	our daily living, dying, rising
Visual	wooden cross painted with scenes of daily life[11]
Text	offered now with Christ

---

[11] E.g., pics.novica.com/pictures/27/p182069_2a_400.jpg. There are many more examples on the web.

Title	asking that we be accepted
Visual	offering figure with *orans* (St. Callistus) [same as topic slide above]
Text #5	Eucharistic Prayer for Reconciliation II: "Holy Father, we humbly beseech you to accept us also, together with your Son . . ." [underline "to accept us together with your Son"]
Title	offering our lives and our world
Visual	offering figure with *orans* [as above]
Text #6	"In the celebration of the Eucharist, these [joys and sorrows of daily life] may most fittingly be offered to the Father along with the body of the Lord. And so, worshipping everywhere by these holy actions, the laity consecrate the world itself to God." (*Lumen Gentium* 34) [underline last portion, beginning with "worshipping . . ."]
Title	our offering taken up
Text #7	"command that these gifts be borne by the hands of your holy angel to your altar on high . . ." (Eucharistic Prayer IV)
Visual	[angel nikē[12] in Catechumenal Hall floor mosaic. if available], or offering figure with *orans* [as above]
Title	to be a living sacrifice with Christ
Visual	offering figure with *orans* [as above]
Text #8	"grant . . . to all who partake of this one Bread and one Chalice that, gathered into one body by the Holy Spirit, they may truly become a living sacrifice in Christ." (Eucharistic Prayer IV) [underline "a living sacrifice in Christ"]
Visual	offering figure with orans [as above, reduced size]
Text #9	"we . . . offer to your glorious majesty from the gifts that you have given us, . . . the holy Bread of eternal life and the Chalice of everlasting salvation." (Eucharistic Prayer I)
Text #10	Prayer over the Gifts, Twentieth Sunday in Ordinary Time [insert entire text, underline from "by offering . . ." to end]

- *For what/whom do we intercede?*

- *To what do we say the great amen?*

[12] Angel of victory, reminiscent of the ancient Greek sculpture, Winged Victory of Samothrace, adapted for the floor mosaic panel about eucharist in the Catechumenal

Recap

Table 6F

Themes	giving thanks for God's saving deeds remembering the two supper commands of Jesus offering the gift of self with Christ making intercession
Title	Thanking, Offering, Interceding
Visual	figure with orans [as above, large]
Text	Catacomb of St. Callistus, third century [below image]

Texts

#1—Preface dialogue (OM 33)

℣. Lift up your hearts.

℟. We lift them up to the Lord.

℣. Let us give thanks to the Lord our God.

℟. It is right and just.

    (preface dialogue)

#2—Eucharistic Prayer III (OM 113)

"Therefore, O Lord, as we celebrate the memorial
of the saving Passion of your Son, . . .
we offer you in thanksgiving
this holy and living sacrifice."
    (Eucharistic Prayer III)

#3—Eucharistic Prayer III (OM 113)

"May he make of us
an eternal offering to you, . . ."
    (Eucharistic Prayer III)

Hall, Aquileia (312–320). Depicted without sword in the mosaic, the angel of victory is
flanked by a basket of bread and a wine goblet that is partially destroyed.

#4—GIRM 79f (also SC 48)

"in this very memorial, the Church, in particular that gathered here and now, offers the unblemished sacrificial Victim in the Holy Spirit to the Father. The Church's intention, indeed, is that the faithful not only offer this unblemished sacrificial Victim but also learn to offer their very selves, and so day by day to be brought, through the mediation of Christ, into unity with God and with each other, so that God may at last be all in all."
(GIRM 79f)

#5—Eucharistic Prayer for Reconciliation II (OM, Appendix to the Order of Mass 7)

"Holy Father, we humbly beseech you
to accept us also, together with your Son . . ."
(Eucharistic Prayer for Reconciliation II)

#6—LG 34[13]

"In the celebration of the Eucharist, these [joys and sorrows of daily life] may most fittingly be offered to the Father along with the body of the Lord. And so, worshipping everywhere by these holy actions, the laity consecrate the world itself to God."
(Vatican II, *Lumen Gentium* 34)

#7—Eucharistic Prayer I (OM 94)

"command that these gifts be borne
by the hands of your holy angel
to your altar on high . . ."
(Eucharistic Prayer I)

#8—Eucharistic Prayer IV (OM 122)

"grant in your loving kindness
to all who partake of this one Bread and one Chalice
that, gathered into one body by the Holy Spirit,
they may truly become a living sacrifice in Christ
to the praise of your glory."
(Eucharistic Prayer IV)

---

[13] Vatican II, *Lumen Gentium: Dogmatic Constitution on the Church* 34.

#9—Eucharistic Prayer I (OM 92)
"we, your servants and your holy people
offer to your glorious majesty
from the gifts that you have given us, . . .
the holy Bread of eternal life
and the Chalice of everlasting salvation."
(Eucharistic Prayer I)

#10—Prayer over the gifts, Twentieth Sunday in Ordinary Time (RM)
"Receive our oblation, O Lord,
by which is brought about a glorious exchange,
that, by offering what you have given,
we may merit to receive your very self."
(Prayer over the gifts, Twentieth Sunday in Ordinary Time)

Reflective Resources

Bernardin, Cardinal Joseph. *Guide for the Assembly*, 16–18. Chicago: Liturgy Training Publications, 1997.

Bernstein, Eleanor, ed. *Liturgical Gestures Words Objects*. Notre Dame, IN: Notre Dame Center for Pastoral Liturgy, 1995.

Hudock, Barry. *The Eucharistic Prayer: A User's Guide*. Collegeville, MN: Liturgical Press. 2010.

Mahony, Cardinal Roger. *Gather Faithfully Together: Guide for Sunday Mass*, 20–25. Chicago: Liturgy Training Publications, 1997.

Ramshaw, Gail. *Words around the Table*. Chicago: Liturgy Training Publications, 1991.

7

Breaking Bread
and Sharing Bread and Cup

Introduction

The Communion rite forms the third part of the Liturgy of the Eucharist. It consists of the following ritual elements:

- Lord's Prayer with its embolism (Deliver us, Lord, . . .)
- prayer for peace and sign of peace
- breaking of bread with acclamation (Lamb of God)
- reception of communion
- prayer after communion

The mystagogy for this session will focus briefly on the Lord's Prayer and then at greater length on the ritual actions of the sign of peace, the breaking of the bread, and the reception of communion. We will then revisit the dialogue of the gift reflected on in chapter 5.

Background Briefing

The Communion rite brings the Liturgy of the Eucharist to completion. The core of the Communion rite consists of preparation rites for and the reception of communion. The preparation rites feature the Lord's Prayer, the sign of peace, and the breaking of the bread. The reception of communion enacts the inner meaning of the Communion rite, namely, that the faithful receive the Body and Blood of the Lord as spiritual food and drink (GIRM 80).

What ritual actions are performed during the Communion rite? The main ritual action is the communion procession; it is set within other actions as well. The standing posture is assumed by all until the invitation to Communion. The presider uses the *orans* gesture for the Lord's Prayer and embolism (expansion on the Lord's Prayer), and that gesture is being imitated increasingly by members of the assembly. They then exchange a sign of peace. The presider breaks the bread as the Lamb of God acclamation is sung. Members of the assembly kneel for the invitation to Communion, approach the altar table in procession to receive it, and kneel in silent reflection after receiving it. All stand for the prayer after Communion. These are the external actions. What is the inner meaning of what we do?

Lord's Prayer

Each element of the Communion rite expresses a facet of that meaning. The Lord's Prayer (Luke 11:2–4) begins: "Father, hallowed be your name." This echoes and recaps the praise and thanks we offered in the first part of the eucharistic prayer as we recalled all that God has done for us. The word "hallow" that comes from Old English can mean "to make holy." God is already holy, so "hallowed" has another meaning in this context. To "hallow" can also mean to "treat as holy, to consider sacred, to venerate." In its biblical context, the word "name" stands for God. In the opening line of the prayer, we pray that God who saves may be held in veneration.

A number of petitions follow that echo the second part of the eucharistic prayer, in which we implore God to continue that saving work. The first petition is the most inclusive of God's saving plan: "Your kingdom come." Among the next petitions, two are especially pertinent for the Communion rite. "Give us each day our daily bread." In the Greek original, the word commonly translated as "daily" is *epiousion*. It is used only twice in the New Testament (Luke 11:3 and Matt 6:11). *Epiousian* is a made-up word not found previously in Greek. Commentators are not certain what it means. Some think it means "sufficient for each day."[1] St. Jerome translated it instead as "supersubstantial" bread, not

---

[1] That is what the translation we now use at Mass suggests.

ordinary daily bread. Eugene LaVerdiere thinks it may simply have meant "our special *epiousian* bread."[2] He suggests that it may simply have been an early Christian way to refer to the Eucharist, before other names such as the "Lord's supper" and the "breaking of bread" became common usage.[3] The next petition prays for an attitude of forgiveness and reconciliation that ought to mark the unity symbolized by sharing at the table of the Lord. "And forgive us our sins, for we ourselves forgive everyone indebted to us"[4] has ethical implications. Paul will later add a powerful motive to that saying of the Lord: "Bear with one another and, if anyone has a complaint against another, forgive each other; just.as the Lord has forgiven you, so you also must forgive" (Col 3:13). Jesus had also instructed his disciples to leave their gift at the altar and first go and be reconciled to their brother or sister who has something against them (Matt 5:23–24).

Sign of peace

Offering the sign of peace follows a prayer for peace and unity. The gift of peace, however, is not meant internally for the church alone. GIRM states: "There follows the Rite of Peace, by which the Church entreats peace and unity for herself and for the whole human family, and the faithful express to each other their ecclesial communion and mutual charity before communicating in the Sacrament" (GIRM 82).

Note especially the first part of that sentence. The gift of Christ's peace is not meant to be a gift we hoard for ourselves alone. Shalom is at the heart of the church's mission. That mission starts with peace-making. When Jesus sent the seventy-two disciples on mission, he gave them this instruction on how to start their proclamation of the reign of God: "Whatever house you enter, first say 'Peace to this house!'" (Luke 10:5). That is the same message of peace the angels used in announcing

---

[2] Perhaps it plays on Jesus' phrase in the bread of life discourse (John 6), "bread from heaven," which in turn evokes the memory of manna in the desert, the special bread God sent from heaven during the exodus.

[3] For a summary of his thought, see Eugene LaVerdiere, *The Eucharist in the New Testament and the Early Church* (Collegeville, MN: Liturgical Press/A Pueblo Book, 1996), 8–10. Note that the latter two names refer to the entire meal. Breaking and sharing bread was the ritual action performed at the beginning of Jewish meals.

[4] Similarly in Luke 6:37: "Forgive, and you will be forgiven."

to the shepherds the birth of the Savior (Luke 2:14). In biblical times the word "peace," *shalom*, meant more than it does now. *Shalom* refers not to a mere absence of fighting, a lull between wars, but to a time that actively promotes the full achievement of all that we humans are able to be. Such a peace that not only avoids violence and conflict but cherishes our differences and supports everyone's development is sorely needed in our neighborhoods and cities, in the Middle East, and in so many other places throughout today's world. The assembly's handshake of peace is a mini-embrace of our hands; it is an iconic statement that "the Church entreats peace and unity for herself and for the whole human family."[5]

Breaking bread, bread broken

The breaking of a small host by the presider, almost hidden from full view of the assembly, seems too small a symbolic gesture to bear much meaning for our lives. But there are deep levels of meaning in the breaking and sharing of the bread, if only we take time to reflect on what we do and how we are to do it liturgically. In chapter 5 we saw that bread is made of grain from the earth transformed into food for human nourishment. It is a human product made for human consumption, our daily staple and the staff of life. It is also a daily means of human bonding and self-giving. Imagine a golden-crusted loaf of bread, fresh from the oven, lying on the table before you.[6] We cannot wait to eat it. It's as though there is a magnetic attraction between us and the bread, drawing the bread to our own body for our nourishment and enjoyment. To take our daily share of bread, break it, and hand it to others to eat is to break the attraction between our body and the bread we instinctively feel is meant for it. "Please have some bread," we say as we offer it to

---

[5] A number of years ago as I was preparing a PowerPoint presentation for a mystagogy of the Eucharist, I chanced upon a compelling image on the web. It showed two hands reaching out to exchange an olive branch. No details about the image were given, but workshop participants and students who saw the image were quickly able to read its meaning. One arm was wearing a short sleeved shirt and a wrist watch; the other had a long sleeve with a cuff beautifully decorated in an eastern style. The unfurnished room in which the exchange was taking place, though not identified, seemed to resemble the Cenacle room in Jerusalem. Viewers quickly glimpsed an image of peace being offered in the war-torn lands of the Bible. Unfortunately, I can no longer find this image on the web.

[6] This reflection is drawn from Edmund Barbotin, *The Humanity of Man*, trans. Matthew J. O"Connell, 378–379 (Maryknoll, NY: Orbis, 1975).

someone. What we are really saying is that we are willing to postpone our own nourishment and put our lives on hold for the sake of the life of another. That is, in its simplest form, an act of human self-giving, an act of self-sacrifice. Life given for the sake of life. It is a most basic human act of loving and caring for another. That is what parents do when they feed their children first.

That is also what Christ does. Eucharistic bread is broken, bread for the life of the world. Life given for the life of another—that is the heart of Christ's sacrifice expressed and enacted in the simple act of breaking and sharing the eucharistic bread. What Christ did, we are to do. And so we approach the table, to receive the body of Christ and become the Body of Christ, and, like him, to be bread for the life of the world.

Bread and justice

But it is not just spiritual nourishment that we are called to provide for others. Let us return for a moment to the meaning of bread on the human level. Table-sharing, anthropologists tell us, is a language. It is one of the most basic languages used by peoples throughout the world. It tells those at table that they are one because they share the same food, one bread.[7] Inclusion of those at the table, however, is only one side of it. Anthropologists also tell us that in fact there is simultaneously an exclusion of those who are not at table, whether unintentional or intentional. Sadly, it is too often the latter. Food can be divisive. It is not only children who fight with food in a school cafeteria. We adults also use food as a weapon, denying it to others by economic embargo or by inequitable distribution and consumption. The Chilean poet Pablo Neruda puts it in stark terms in a poem entitled "The Great Tablecloth." He describes a sumptuous feast at a fiesta going on down the lane from a wheat field and, in contrast, the experience of a poor farmworker in that field. The following searing lines name the peasant's experience:

> The peasant in the field ate
> his poor quota of bread,
> he was alone, it was late,
> he was surrounded by wheat,

---

[7] Paul enunciated that same principle in 1 Cor 10:17: "Because there is one bread, we who are many are one body, for we all partake of the one bread."

but he had no more bread;
he ate it with grim teeth,
looking at it with hard eyes.

. . .

Eating alone is a disappointment,
but not eating matters more,
is hollow and green, has thorns
like a chain of fish-hooks
trailing from the heart,
clawing at your insides.

Hunger feels like pincers,
like the bite of crabs,
it burns and has no fire.
Hunger is a cold fire.
Let us sit down to eat
with all those who haven't eaten;
let us spread great tablecloths,
put salt in the lakes of the world,
set up planetary bakeries,
tables with strawberries in snow,
and a plate like the moon itself
from which we can all eat.

For now I ask no more
than the justice of eating.[8]

We cannot disconnect eucharistic feasting from that other kind of human eating. It is a matter of justice, the "justice of eating." The words of Jesus in the parable of the last judgment disallow such a disconnect. One criterion for who will or will not inherit the kingdom is clear. "I was hungry and you gave me food . . ." / "I was hungry and you gave me no food . . ." (Matt 25:35, 42). In keeping with the Lord's command about loving our enemies, Paul writes bluntly: "if your enemies are hungry, feed them" (Rom 12:20). Catholic tradition has long counted feeding the hungry among the corporal works of mercy. A strand of French theology insists that reception of the Eucharist ought to call us to repentance for the ways that we exclude other humans from their share of daily

[8] Excerpts from "The Great Tablecloth," *Pablo Neruda: Extravagaria*, trans. Alastair Reid (New York: Farrar, Straus and Giroux, 1974), 45 and 47.

bread. Cardinal Bernardin called our small unleavened host a "bread of the poor;" it is a "hungry bread." It can serve to remind us not only of our need to be fed again and again by the Eucharist but also of our responsibility outside of Mass to attend to the "justice of eating" we owe to those who are hungry and have no bread. Coming to the aid of others in need, to be "good Samaritans," is a basic part of our mission as disciples.

To repeat, what Christ did, we are to do. And so we approach the table to receive the body of Christ and become the Body of Christ, and, like him, to be bread for the life of the world. Our approach to the table takes the form of a procession, accompanied by song. Unlike the entrance procession in which only "a representative few" walk, in this procession we are all invited to walk. It is "journey distilled," the lifelong journey of coming to the table to receive bread for the journey. That journey began for us with the initiatory sacraments and reached completion in our reception of our First Holy Communion. The journey will reach its culmination at the doorstep of eternity when we receive the Holy Communion we call *Viaticum*, literally food for the journey from earthly life into eternal life. Each reception of communion during our earthly journey to that last day should bear both a faint remembrance of our First Communion and a veiled anticipation of our reception of *Viaticum* before death. We come to receive the body of Christ, that we may be the Body of Christ, that he may be with us and walk with us on the way.

Communion

The act of receiving Christ in communion is the fullest symbol of our participation in the Eucharist.[9] It is also a simple gesture. We stretch out our hands, as a fourth-century mystagogue instructs the newly baptized, to make of them a throne to receive the King. The eucharistic minister offers the host, saying: "The Body of Christ." We answer, "Amen." "Body of Christ" is a phrase that has two references in St. Paul's First Letter to the Corinthians:

> The cup of blessing that we bless, is it not a sharing in the blood of Christ? The bread that we break, is it not a sharing in the body of Christ? Because there is one bread, we who are many are one body, for we all partake of the one bread. (1 Cor 10:16)

---

[9] GIRM 13 intimates that all in the assembly should receive communion at every Mass.

> I received from the Lord what I also handed on to you, that
> the Lord Jesus on the night when he was betrayed took a loaf
> of bread, and when he had given thanks, he broke it and said,
> "This is my body that is for you. Do this in remembrance of
> me. (1 Cor 11:23–24)

The first passage refers to Christ's Body that is the church, the second
to his body given sacramentally in the Eucharist.

Following the thought of St. Paul (1 Cor 10–11), St. Augustine reminds us that we say a double "Amen." We say "Amen" both to the body
of Christ given to us sacramentally and to the Body of Christ that is the
church.[10] In saying this "Amen" to the one who is the Bread of Life,
we also commit ourselves to being and living as the Body of Christ in
the world, to being bread for others, within the church and beyond it.
Augustine's thought is beautifully enshrined in the prayer we say after
communion on his feast:

> May partaking of Christ's table
> sanctify us, we pray, O Lord,
> that, being made members of his Body,
> we may become what we have received.[11]

We will follow up on being bread for others in the next chapter, on
being sent, and in the final chapter we will revisit the "Amen" we say
throughout the Mass.

Table and vessels

Two reflective poems on table and vessels can help us savor the inner
meaning of the Communion rite.

Altar Table

Banquet table
table of the Lord
table of the Lord's people
open to all, ready for all
    Jew/Greek

---

[10] See St. Augustine, *Sermon* 272.
[11] Prayer after Communion in the *Roman Missal* for August 28, St. Augustine,

slave/free
male/female
Come, sit at the "welcome table"
free seating for all
no reserved seats
no partiality
no discrimination.
"You are all one in Christ Jesus."[12]

Cup & Plate

Chalice cup and paten
fashioned from earth's core
fire-tried
molded
shaped for sacrament.
Earth's creatures
reaching out to hold
divinity.
Human vessels with
broken bread;
wine spilled out
Christ among his people.[13]

Communion under both kinds

One final question is suggested by the pairing of "broken bread" and "wine spilled out" in the above poetic reflection. Why is receiving communion under both kinds important? At the Last Supper Jesus invited his disciples to both eat and drink. GIRM 281 gives us this additional rationale: "Holy Communion has a fuller form as a sign when it is distributed under both kinds. For in this form the sign of the Eucharistic banquet is more clearly evident and clear expression is given to the divine will by which the new and eternal Covenant is ratified in the Blood of the Lord, as also the relationship between the Eucharistic banquet and the eschatological banquet in the Father's kingdom."

[12] William G. Storey, "Altar Table," LWGO, 51.
[13] Estelle Martin, RSM, "Cup & Plate," LGWO, 53.

Dialogue of the gift II

The liturgical dialogue of the gift reaches fulfillment in the act of communion. In response to God's gift of creation and our calling to be "fellow workers" with God in creation, we have brought our work, our lives, and our world with us into the assembly at the beginning of the celebration. We have then brought them to the table in the presentation of the gifts, placing them on the altar in spirit and dedicating them for the offering to come. In the eucharistic prayer, we have celebrated the memorial of God's gift of salvation to us in the life, death, and resurrection of Christ. In response we then offered to God the gift of ourselves as a "holy and living sacrifice" in union with Christ's self-gift. The liturgical dialogue of the gift between God and us reaches fulfillment and is sealed in the act of communion, in which "each give the self to the other."[14] And so, in the prayer after Communion for Thursday within the Octave of Easter we pray:

> Hear, O Lord, our prayers,
> that this most holy exchange,
> by which you have redeemed us,
> may bring your help in this present life,
> and ensure for us the joys of eternal gladness.

This holy exchange of receiving and giving is not meant to end with the Communion rite, however. It ought to spiral out into our daily lives and expand outward to draw in those around us. The example of the early church is instructive. St. Justin the Martyr recounts that the collection was taken up after communion and used for widows, orphans, prisoners, strangers, and all those in need.[15] A dim memory of this early practice is enshrined in our current directive for the celebration of the Lord's Supper on Holy Thursday evening. If a collection is taken up, the rubrics tell us, it is to be used for those who are in need.[16] It is not meant for the support of the local community, as on other Sundays of the year. The dialogue of the gift cannot be a closed circle; it must spiral out beyond the celebration. Taking up the collection after communion in the time of St. Justin made that connection crystal clear. The assembly itself is sent

---

[14] Miller, "Presentation of gifts," 36.

[15] Justin Martyr, *Apology* I, 67 (c. 150); full text quoted in the interlude after chapter 3.

[16] OM 14, Thursday of the Lord's Supper.

from communion back into lives of self-giving love and service in world. Having received God's gift of self, we are to give ourselves to others.

The Mystagogy

Setting the stage

The environment for this session could feature a loaf of bread and a flagon of red wine, also a ceramic cup and plate, artistically arranged and flanked by candles. Inviting participants to break and share the loaf of bread, as well as a bit of wine, might be an appropriate way to conclude the reflective walk-through.

Table 7A

Topic slide for PowerPoint[17]	
Title	Breaking Bread and Sharing Bread and Cup
Visuals	loaf of bread and goblet of red wine

Attending to experience

- *What do we do as part of the Communion rite?*

Table 7B

Elicit the elements in detail

- *In a moment of silence, remember and relive those things.*
- *Name aloud the elements you love the most in the Communion rite.*
- *Which elements help you best to enter into this rite? Why?*

Ritual actions and symbols

Lord's Prayer

- *Which phrases in the Lord's Prayer do you like best? Why?*

---

[17] The material in the tables is offered as a resource for facilitators who wish to use PowerPoint. The cells (rows) between darker lines in each table represent individual sample slides. The mystagogy can be conducted using only the starter questions and live interaction, if the facilitator so wishes.

Table 7C

Theme	Lord's Prayer: praise and petitions
Title	Lord's Prayer: praise
Visual	Jesus teaching (stained glass) or praying (stained glass)
Text	"hallowed be your name"
Title	Lord's Prayer: petitions
Visual	Jesus teaching (stained glass) or praying (stained glass)
Texts	"your kingdom come" [add and comment one by one:] "give us each day our daily bread" "forgive us our sins"

- *Why is it called **the** Christian prayer?*
- *What connection is there between the Lord's Prayer and Communion?*

Sign of peace

- *How is the sign of peace given in this community?*
- *What does the physical gesture (handshake, bow, embrace) mean in ordinary life?*
- *What does it mean at this point in the Mass?*
- *What do we think peace is in our world?*
- *What is the meaning of the peace we exchange at Mass?*
- *To whom should we extend that peace?*

Table 7D

Themes	meaning of peace/shalom; meaning of the sign of peace offering peace the first act of mission [72 disciples]
Title	Sign of Peace
Visual	handshake of peace (close-up) or a mutual bow
Text #1	"the Church entreats peace and unity for herself and for the whole human family" (GIRM 82)

Breaking of bread

- *What does breaking/sharing bread with your family and friends mean?*

Table 7E

Themes	meaning of sharing bread with family, friends food-sharing as language Barbotin: life put on hold for sake of another's life (= sacrifice)
Title	Breaking Bread
Visuals	family at table (local community?) breaking bread into another's hands (close-up)
Text	life put on hold for sake of another's life

- *What is the symbolism of the presider visibly breaking the host at Mass?*

Table 7F

Themes	Jesus: bread broken and given "for the life of the world" "one body because we eat of the one loaf"
Title	Breaking Bread
Visual	broken loaf of bread (close-up)
Texts	"He broke the bread and gave it to them."

- *Does the breaking of bread at Mass say anything about world hunger and justice?*

Table 7G

Themes	feeding the hungry multitudes (six accounts in Scripture!) Jesus' example of inclusive dining Neruda: "The Great Tablecloth"
Title	Expression of Unity
Text #2	"Because there is one bread, we who are many are one body, for we all partake of the one bread." (2 Cor 10:17)
Text	sometimes used to exclude
Text #3	Neruda, "The Great Tablecloth" [read and insert final line:] "For now I ask no more than the justice of eating."
Text	call to repentance
Title	Expression of Inclusion
Visual	view of altar from behind assembly (local community)

Text #4	"Altar Table" [read entire poem, post individual phrases being read] "free seating for all/no reserved seats/no partiality/no discrimination"
Title	Expression of Service
Visual	multiplication of loaves (fresco, Catacomb of Priscilla)
Text	"you give them something to eat"
Text	"This man welcomes sinners and eats with them." (Luke 15:1–2)
Title	Expression of Self-sacrifice
Visual	close up of fraction of the host
Text #5	"The bread that I will give for the life of the world is my flesh." (John 6:51)

Reception of communion

- *What does processing to Communion mean?*

Table 7H

Themes	bread for the journey between first Communion and *Viaticum*
Title	Processing
Visual	communion procession (local community)
Text	to receive bread for the journey
Text	"journey distilled"

- *How do we show reverence? To what do we say "Amen" as we receive Communion?*

Table 7I

Themes	showing reverence two meanings of "Body of Christ. Amen" (1 Cor 10–11)
Title	Showing Reverence
Visual	communicant's hands outstretched (close-up)
Text #6	"Stretch out your hands, making the left hand a throne for the right hand, which receives the King." (fourth-century instruction to the newly baptized)

Title	Saying "Amen"
Visual	host offered to communicant (close-up, local community)
Text #7	"Body of Christ." "Amen."
Title	A double "Amen"
Text #8	Augustine, Sermon 272 (insert full text and attribute)
Title	One Body, Fed by His Body
Text #9	"grant that we . . . may become one body, one Spirit in Christ." (Eucharistic Prayer III)

- *What is the meaning of receiving Communion under both kinds?*

Table 7J

Themes	Lord's command to eat and drink "fuller form as a sign" (GIRM 281)
Title	Receiving
Visual	ceramic cup & plate
Text #10	Cup and Plate poem [read]

- *Why do we sing a song during the reception of Communion?*
- *Why is there a time of silence after Communion?*

Table 7K

Themes	"praise and pray to God in their hearts" (GIRM 45)
Title	Communion with Christ
Visual	people kneeling in silence (local community)
Text	"I am with you always." (Matt 28:20)

Recap

Table 7L

Themes	breaking bread communion procession "Body of Christ. Amen." dialogue of the gift
Text #11	Prayer after Communion [insert full text, then underline "holy exchange"]
Title	The dialogue of the gift continues
Title	Breaking Bread, Sharing Bread and Cup
Visuals	several images repeated from above

Texts

#1—GIRM 82

"[T]he Church entreats peace and unity for herself and for the whole human family. . . ." (GIRM 82)

#2—2 Cor 10:16–17

"The cup of blessing that we bless, is it not a sharing in the blood of Christ? The bread that we break, is it not a sharing in the body of Christ? Because there is one bread, we who are many are one body, for we all partake of the one bread."
(2 Cor 10:16–17)

#3—Neruda, "The Great Tablecloth"[18]

The peasant in the field ate
his poor quota of bread,
he was alone, it was late,
he was surrounded by wheat,
but he had no more bread;
he ate it with grim teeth,
looking at it with hard eyes.

---

[18] Excerpts from *Pablo Neruda:Extravagaria*, trans. Alastair Reid (New York: Farrar, Straus and Giroux, 1974), 45 and 47.

. . .

Eating alone is a disappointment,
but not eating matters more,
is hollow and green, has thorns
like a chain of fish-hooks
trailing from the heart,
clawing at your insides.

Hunger feels like pincers,
like the bite of crabs,
it burns and has no fire.
Hunger is a cold fire.
Let us sit down to eat
with all those who haven't eaten;
let us spread great tablecloths,
put salt in the lakes of the world,
set up planetary bakeries,
tables with strawberries in snow,
and a plate like the moon itself
from which we can all eat.

For now I ask no more
than the justice of eating.
> (Neruda, "The Great Tablecloth")

#4—"Altar Table," by William G. Storey (LGWO, 53)
Banquet table
table of the Lord
table of the Lord's people
open to all, ready for all
  Jew/Greek
  slave/free
  male/female
Come, sit at the "welcome table"
  free seating for all
  no reserved seats
  no partiality
  no discrimination.
"You are all one in Christ Jesus."
> (William G. Storey)

#5—John 6:51

"The bread that I will give for the life of the world is my flesh."
(John 6:51)

#6—Fourth-century catechumenal instruction to the newly baptized

"Stretch out your hands, making the left hand a throne for the
right hand, which receives the King."
(Cyril of Jerusalem[19])

#7—Distribution of communion (OM 134)

"The Body of Christ. Amen."
(*Roman Missal*)

#8—St. Augustine, Sermon 272[20]

"If then you are the body of Christ and his members, it is your
sacrament that reposes on the altar of the Lord. It is your sacrament
which you receive. You answer 'Amen' to what you yourselves are
and in answering you are enrolled. You answer 'Amen' to the words
'The body of Christ.' Be, then, a member of the body of Christ to
verify your 'Amen.'"
(St. Augustine, Sermon 272)

#9—Eucharistic Prayer III (OM 113)

"[G]rant that we, who are nourished
by the Body and Blood of your Son
and filled with his Holy Spirit,
may become one body, one spirit in Christ."
(Eucharistic Prayer III)

#10—"Cup & Plate," by Estelle Martin, RSM (LGWO, 53)

Chalice cup and paten
fashioned from earth's core

---

[19] Cyril of Jerusalem, *Fifth Mystagogical Catechesis*, 21.

[20] Text as translated in *The Mass: Ancient Liturgies and Patristic Texts*, ed. André Hamman. OFM, (New York: Alba House, 1967), 207.

fire-tried
molded
shaped for sacrament.
Earth's creatures
reaching out to hold
divinity.
Human vessels with
broken bread;
wine spilled out
Christ among his people.
        (Estelle Martin)

#11—Prayer after Communion (RM, Thursday in Easter Week)

Hear, O Lord, our prayers,
that this most holy exchange,
by which you have redeemed us,
may bring your help in this present life
and ensure for us eternal gladness.
        (prayer after communion, Thursday in Easter Week)

Supplementary text

#12—Prayer after communion (RM, August 28, St. Augustine)

May partaking of Christ's table
sanctify us, we pray, O Lord,
that, being made members of his Body,
we may become what we have received.
        (prayer after communion, August 28)

Reflective Resources

Bernardin, Cardinal Joseph. *Guide for the Assembly*, 19–21. Chicago: Liturgy
    Training Publications, 1997.

Bernstein, Eleanor, ed. *Liturgical Gestures Words Objects*. Notre Dame, IN:
    Notre Dame Center for Pastoral Liturgy, 1995.

Mahony, Cardinal Roger. *Gather Faithfully Together: Guide for Sunday Mass*,
    20–25. Chicago: Liturgy Training Publications, 1997.

Ramshaw, Gail. *Words around the Table*. Chicago: Liturgy Training Publi-
    cations, 1991.

8

Being Sent

Introduction

The concluding rites of the Mass are very brief. They consist of the following ritual elements:

- greeting
- blessing
- dismissal
- reverence of the altar

The mystagogy for this session will focus on the dismissal.

Background Briefing[1]

The core of the concluding rites is the final blessing and the dismissal. The purpose of the dismissal of the people, GIRM 90 states, is "that each may go back to doing good works, praising and blessing God." To use a human analogy, these rites are similar to our response to any experience that has moved us deeply, like a live experience of a moving musical performance or the victory of our favorite sports team. We know that it has been a gift, a blessing, and we resolve to take it with us in the form of memory and keepsakes. Think, for example, of

---

[1] This briefing repeats and expands what I have written in "A Mystagogy of the Eucharist," *Liturgical Ministry* 20 (Fall 2011): 165–166.

our joy over a wonderful sight-seeing tour and the pictures, stories, and souvenirs we bring back to share with others. In the concluding rites of the Mass, we acknowledge that God has blessed us with the holy gift we have celebrated, and we accept our responsibility to take it with us and live it out: "Go and announce the Gospel of the Lord;" "Go in peace, glorifying the Lord by your life." "Thanks be to God."

A charge

Though the concluding rites are very brief and deceptively simple, the meaning of the dismissal in particular runs far deeper. Cardinal Bernardin comments in a wonderful mystagogical turn of phrase: "The dismissal of the assembly is *like the breaking of the bread*. We have become 'the bread of life' and the 'cup of blessing' for the world. Now we are scattered, broken, poured out to be life for the world. What happens at home, at work, at meals? What do we make of our time, our words, our deeds, our resources of all kinds? That is what matters."[2] In a similar vein Pope John Paul II has written: "The dismissal at the end of each Mass is a *charge* given to Christians, inviting them to work for the spread of the Gospel and the imbuing of society with Christian values."[3]

We ought not underestimate the great dignity and utter seriousness of that charge for Christians. We are sent to carry out the mission of Christ even beyond the boundaries of Christianity. Scripture scholar Leslie Newbigin has written that "Christians are a hermeneutic of the Gospel, and for many people it's the only Gospel they'll ever read."[4] Similarly, Pope John XXIII is reported to have once said: "The Christian is the eighth sacrament and the only sacrament that the non-believer will ever receive."[5]

Sent on mission

The sending has to do with the missionary nature of the church. Jesus' final words to his disciples were: "Go therefore and make disciples of all

---

[2] Bernardin, *Guide for the Assembly*, 23, no.79, emphasis added.

[3] John Paul II, *Mane nobiscum Domine* 24 (emphasis original). Online at www.vatican .va/holy_father/john_paul_ii/apost_letters/documents/hf_jp-ii_apl_20041008_mane -nobiscum-domine_en.html.

[4] Leslie Newbigin, *The Gospel in a Pluralistic Society* (Grand Rapids, MI: William B. Eerdmans, 1989), 227.

[5] Pope John XXIII, cited on several websites, no source given.

nations, baptizing them in the name of the Father and of the Son and of the Holy Spirit, and teaching them to obey everything that I have commanded you" (Matt 28:19–20). The Latin for dismissal, *Ite, missa est,* can be translated either as "Go, the Mass is ended" or as "Go, you are sent." Choosing the latter rendition, Pope Benedict XVI has written: "These few words succinctly express the missionary nature of the Church. The People of God might be helped to understand more clearly this essential dimension of the Church's life, taking the dismissal as a starting-point."[6]

The two versions of the dismissal added in the recently revised Roman Missal (OM 144) also stress this missionary function: "Go and announce the Gospel of the Lord," and "Go in peace, glorifying the Lord by your life." In the words of a faculty colleague, Anthony J. Gittins, disciples are those who are called to be sent, who are co-missioned along with Jesus. He was sent to bring into the world the total and unconditional self-giving love of God.[7] That is our mission too.

Silent proclamation

The primary mission on which today's disciples are sent at the conclusion of each eucharistic celebration has been described in church documents as a "silent proclamation" of the Gospel. This we do by the wordless witness of our lives. In an apostolic exhortation of 1975, Pope Paul VI gave a stirring description of how this silent proclamation is carried out.

> Take a Christian or a handful of Christians who, in the midst of their own community, show their capacity for understanding and acceptance, their sharing of life and destiny with other people, their solidarity with the efforts of all for whatever is noble and good. Let us suppose that, in addition, they radiate in an altogether simple and unaffected way their faith in values that go beyond current values, and their hope in something that is not seen and that one would not dare to imagine. Through this wordless witness these Christians stir up irresistible questions in the hearts of those who see how they live: Why are they like this?

---

[6] Benedict XVI, *Sacramentum Caritatis* 51. Online at www.vatican.va/holy_father /benedict_xvi/apost_exhortations/documents/hf_ben-xvi_exh_20070222_sacramentum -caritatis_en.html.

[7] Anthony J. Gittins, *Called to Be Sent: Co-Missioned as Disciples Today* (Liguori, MO: Liguori Publications, 2008).

Why do they live in this way? What or who is it that inspires them? Why are they in our midst? Such a witness is already a silent proclamation of the Good News and a very powerful and effective one. Here we have an initial act of evangelization.[8]

The liturgical dismissal, then, sends us back into our life-mission, to what Ion Bria has called "the liturgy after the liturgy,"[9] or others "the liturgy of the neighbor." Karl Rahner has offered a similar image when he speaks of the dying and rising that takes place in daily life in the world as the "liturgy of the world." Liturgy and life flow into each other in a dynamic interchange. The reflections of Rahner and Bria provide a helpful framework for understanding that interchange, and they deserve further thought.[10]

Life as liturgy

Let's look first at the reflection developed by Karl Rahner.[11] In the old understanding of sacrament, particularly the Eucharist, humans had to leave the secular, profane world (the Latin root *pro-fanum* literally means outside the temple), where God is distant, in order for them to enter the temple (*fanum*). Only there, in the temple, could God be encountered as present and saving. In the new understanding of sacrament, according to Rahner, the God who was with the Israelites on the exodus journey is also present everywhere in the world, a world permeated to its depths by God's grace. The history of the world, Rahner says, is a terrible and sublime history of dying and rising, in ways small and large. That history reached its fulfillment in the dying and rising of Christ, in which we are all joined in our daily moments of dying and rising, however small they may be. Rahner

---

[8] Paul VI, *Evangelii Nuntiandi* 21. Online at www.vatican.va/holy_father/paul_vi /apost_exhortations/documents/hf_p-vi_exh_19751208_evangelii-nuntiandi_en.html.

[9] Ion Bria, "The Liturgy after the Liturgy." Online at www.rondtbmsk.ru/info/en/ Brian_en.htm; also *The Liturgy after the Liturgy: Mission and Witness from an Orthodox Perspective* (Geneva: WCC Publications, 1996), 19–35.

[10] The following two paragraphs are taken with some editing from my article, "Eucharist as Memorial," from the *Dictionary of the Passion*, ed. Robin Ryan (Rome: Città Nuova, forthcoming in several languages).

[11] Karl Rahner, "Considerations on the Active Role of the Person in the Sacramental Event," *Theological Investigations* XIV, trans. David Bourke (New York: Seabury, 1976), 161–184.

calls that history "the liturgy of the world." Liturgy in the narrow sense, then, the liturgy that takes place in church, is no more than a small sign, an *anamnesis*, in which we remember and interpret the liturgy of the world we have experienced. That liturgy of the world is hidden and not always apparent amid the preoccupations, responsibilities, and complexities of daily living. We need the church liturgy to help us name and interpret it.

The second reflection was developed by Ion Bria.[12] Drawing on recent theological discussion within Orthodox Christianity about the relation of ecclesiology and missiology, Bria speaks of life in the world as "the liturgy after the liturgy." The faithful are sent from the liturgy of the church into daily life to offer a liturgy of service and love on behalf of others. Some have also called this the "liturgy of the neighbor," or the "liturgy offered on the altar of the neighbor's heart." There is continuity and unity between these two liturgies, one offered in church liturgy, the other lived out in Christian life.

We may not be accustomed to thinking of the daily dying and rising we experience in our lives as liturgy. We need only look to the life of Jesus whom we follow to find another, unexpected way of thinking. Edward Schillebeeckx notes that Jesus did not give his life in a solemn liturgical ritual. It was an execution, a secular event that took place outside the walls of Jerusalem, not in the temple. He was not a Levite or priest, authorized in Jewish law to offer cultic sacrifice. Nonetheless we consider his death the supreme act of worship. Jesus' gift of his life summed up in death on the cross gives new meaning to a Christian life of giving oneself. Here is what Schillebeeckx writes:

> Calvary was not a Church liturgy, but an hour of human life, which Jesus experienced as worship. In it our redemption is to be found. We have not been redeemed by an act of pure worship, a liturgical service—our redemption was accomplished by an act which was part of Jesus' human life, situated in history and in the world. . . . It is possible to speak of a secular liturgy. . . . In this way the new concept of worship came into being—human life itself experienced as a liturgy or as worship of God. Cult thus acquired a new meaning in the New Testament—life in the world shared with one's fellow-men must itself be a "spiritual

---

[12] Ion Bria, as above in footnote 9; also: "The Liturgy after the Liturgy," *International Review of Mission* 67 (Jan 1978): 86–90.

sacrifice." On the basis of Jesus' self-sacrifice, the Christian's
life in this world can now become worship.[13]

In the early church, this idea of life being a living, spiritual sacrifice
was used primarily for Christian life (see Rom 12:1; 1 Pet 2:5; Heb
13:15). In Rahner's words, the liturgy of the church is a small sign, the
anamnesis and interpretation of the liturgy of the world, our dying and
rising in daily life.

If initation into the mystery of Christ's dying and rising (CCC 1075)
is the goal of both liturgy and catechesis, and if, with St. Paul, we see
Christian life as a journey of dying and rising with Christ day by day
(see 2 Cor 4:10), then both liturgical celebration and reflection on its
interpretation of Christian life ought to move us closer to that goal.
Christians are called to become a living spiritual sacrifice, offering a
lifetime of "secular worship" in imitation of Christ. That is the mission
to which we are sent into the world, to be Christ to the world. Teresa
of Avila (1515–1582) beautifully expresses this in the following poem:

> Christ has no body but yours,
> No hands, no feet on earth but yours,
> Yours are the eyes with which he looks
> Compassion on this world,
> Yours are the feet with which he walks to do good,
> Yours are the hands, with which he blesses all the world.
> Yours are the hands, yours are the feet,
> Yours are the eyes, you are his body.
> Christ has no body now but yours,
> No hands, no feet on earth but yours,
> Yours are the eyes with which he looks
> compassion on this world.
> Christ has no body now on earth but yours.[14]

Recap

These reflections offer a way to recap a major thread of thought that
has run through all these background briefings. What we celebrate in the

---

[13] Edward Schillebeeckx, *God the Future of Man*, trans. N. D. Smith (New York: Sheed
and Ward, 1968), 99–100.

[14] Online at www.journeywithjesus.net/PoemsAndPrayers/Teresa_Of_Avila_Christ_Has
_No_Body.shtml.

liturgy in Word and sacrament is to be lived out in our lives before and after the liturgy. The entrance procession forms a bridge for Christians to move from life to liturgy. In the entrance rite, a processional cross, candles, and the Book of the Gospels held aloft lead the way. The heart of Christian life in the world is summed up in these ritual symbols. Our daily dying and rising lived out in the world are brought into the assembly. The cross is the story of Jesus, to be taken up daily by any who would follow him (Luke 9:23). The candles tell of the silent witness of those called to be the light of the world (Matt 5:14–16), following the One who is the Light of the World (John 8:12). The Book of the Gospels tells the story of those who are willing, like Jesus, to lose their lives in loving service for his sake and the sake of the Gospel (Mark 8:35). We should all walk—in spirit if not in fact—in that procession into the assembly, carrying with us our daily work, our lives, and our world as our liturgy of the world.[15] Then at the presentation of the bread and wine, the condensed symbols of our work, ourselves, and our world, we should also walk in spirit to place our gift on the altar table for the offering that is to follow. In that pivotal moment of the eucharistic prayer (the *anamnesis*), we unite that offering of ourselves with the self-offering of Christ. And then, nourished by Christ's gift of himself to us, we are sent back into the world to live out the liturgy of life, each striving in our own way to be bread for the life of the world. The dismissal and departure are the bridge from the liturgy back into that world.[16] The greeting before the dismissal assures us that we do not go alone; "The Lord be with you." We are sent to be his image and presence in our world.

When we gather again, it is that liturgy of life from which we return and that we bring back to the liturgy of the Eucharist. Reflecting on the words of Pope Benedict cited above, Gregory Pierce counsels us to think of the gathering not simply as a coming together, as though it were for the first time, but rather as a return from mission.[17] With that, the cycle between liturgy and life is completed, a cycle, or better, a spiral

---

[15] This understanding of human life as a liturgy is graphically portrayed in the painted crosses in Spanish-speaking cultures. Painted on the cross are scenes from every aspect of human life and work. Images of this abound on the web.

[16] Eileen D. Crowley, a faculty colleague, suggests that above the main door as we go out there should be a sign saying "servant entrance."

[17] Gregory F. Augustine Pierce, *The Mass Is Never Ended: Rediscovering Our Mission to Transform the World* (Notre Dame, IN: Ave Maria Press, 2007), 42–43.

that grows and deepens, ready to be repeated again and again. Surely, then, the gathering and sending rites, the indispensable liturgical bridge by which we move back and forth between liturgy and Christian life, deserve our full pastoral care.[18]

The Mystagogy

Setting the stage

The environment for this session could feature the community's processional cross in its stand and the Book of the Gospels enshrined and flanked by candles. Inviting participants to approach and venerate the cross by touch or bow would be fitting either when appropriate during the session, or at the conclusion of the reflective walk-through.

Table 8A

Topic slide for PowerPoint[19]	
Title	Being Sent
Visual	Presider's hand raised in blessing (close-up) or: "Go Make Disciples" with attribution (Giselle Bauche)

Attending to experience

- *What do we do as part of the concluding rite?*

Table 8B

Elicit the elements in detail

- *In a moment of silence, remember and relive those things.*
- *Name aloud the elements you love the most.*
- *Which elements help you best to understand what the dismissal means?*

[18] E.g., would it not make sense to enshrine cross and Book of the Gospels in the narthex for people to venerate both as they enter the assembly to celebrate Eucharist and as they are sent from it to go back out on mission?

[19] The material in the tables is offered as a resource for facilitators who wish to use PowerPoint. The cells (rows) between darker lines in each table represent individual sample slides. The mystagogy can be conducted using only the starter questions and live interaction, if the facilitator so wishes.

Ritual actions and symbols

Table 8C

Themes	blessing mission life as liturgy
Title	Dismissal
Text #1	Bernardin: "The Dismissal . . ." (Bernardin, Guide for the Assembly, no 79) [insert entire text, then underline "Like the breaking of the bread"]
Title	Called to be sent
Text #2	Benedict XVI: "Ite, missa est . . ." (Benedict XVI, *Sacramentum Caritatis* 51) [insert entire text, then underline "taking the dismissal as a starting-point."]
Title	Sent on mission
Visuals	"Go Make Disciples"
Text	(Gisele Bauche) [attribution below image]
Title	Sent to spread the Gospel
Text #3	John Paul II: "The dismissal . . ." (John Paul II, *Mane nobiscum Domine* 24) [insert entire text, then underline "a charge given to Christians"]
Title	Sent to give witness
Text #4a	Paul VI: "Take a Christian . . . dare to imagine." (more) [insert this part of the text]
Title	by silent proclamation
Text #4b	Paul VI: "Through this wordless witness . . . act of evangelization." (Paul VI, *Evangelii Nuntiandi* 21) [insert rest of the text, then underline the phrases "wordless witness" and "Such a witness is already a silent proclamation"]
Title	Sent to consecrate the world
Text #5	Vatican II, LG: "In the celebration . . ." (Vatican II, Constitution on the Church 34) [insert entire text, then underline the phrases "worshipping everywhere by these holy actions" and "the laity consecrate the world itself to God"]
Title	The Christian Calling

| Text #6 | Newbigin [insert entire text with abbreviated reference] |
| Text #7 | John XXIII [insert entire text with attribution] |

Recap

Table 8D

Themes	sent on mission
Title	Being sent
Visual	"Go Make Disciples" with attribution (Giselle Bauche)

Texts

#1—Bernardin, *Guide for the Assembly*, 79

"The dismissal of the assembly is like the breaking of the bread. We have become 'the bread of life' and the 'cup of blessing' for the world. Now we are scattered, broken, poured out to be life for the world. What happens at home, at work, at meals? What do we make of our time, our words, our deeds, our resources of all kinds? That is what matters."

(Bernardin, *Guide for the Assembly*, 79)

#2—Benedict XVI

"*Ite, missa est.* These few words succinctly express the missionary nature of the Church. The People of God might be helped to understand more clearly this essential dimension of the Church's life, taking the dismissal as a starting-point."

(Benedict XVI, *Sacramentum Caritatis* 51)

#3—John Paul II

"The dismissal at the end of each Mass is a *charge* given to Christians, inviting them to work for the spread of the Gospel and the imbuing of society with Christian values."

(John Paul II, *Mane nobiscum Domine* 24)

#4—Paul VI, *Evangelii Nuntiandi* 21

"Take a Christian or a handful of Christians who, in the midst of their own community, show their capacity for understanding and acceptance, their sharing of life and destiny with other people, their solidarity with the efforts of all for whatever is noble and good. Let us suppose that, in addition, they radiate in an altogether simple and unaffected way their faith in values that go beyond current values, and their hope in something that is not seen and that one would not dare to imagine. Through this wordless witness these Christians stir up irresistible questions in the hearts of those who see how they live: Why are they like this? Why do they live in this way? What or who is it that inspires them? Why are they in our midst? Such a witness is already a silent proclamation of the Good News and a very powerful and effective one. Here we have an initial act of evangelization."

(Paul VI, *Evangelii Nuntiandi* 21)

#5—Vatican II, LG

"In the celebration of the Eucharist, these [joys and sorrows of daily life] may most fittingly be offered to the Father along with the body of the Lord. And so, worshipping everywhere by these holy actions, the laity consecrate the world itself to God."

(Vatican II, *Dogmatic Constitution on the Church* 34)

#6—Newbigin

"Christians are a hermeneutic of the Gospel, and for many people it's the only Gospel they'll ever read."[20]
(Newbigin, *The Gospel in a Pluralist Society*, 227)

#7—John XXIII

"Christians are the eighth sacrament and the only sacrament non-believers can receive."[21]

---

[20] Leslie Newbigin, *The Gospel in a Pluralist Society*, 227.

[21] Attributed to Pope John XXIII on a number of websites, such as www.officefor pastoralservices.org/resources/worship_%20sacraments.pdf.

Reflective Resources

Bernardin, Cardinal Joseph. *Guide for the Assembly*, 22–23. Chicago: Liturgy Training Publications, 1997.

Bernstein, Eleanor, ed. *Liturgical Gestures Words Objects*. Notre Dame, IN: Notre Dame Center for Pastoral Liturgy, 1995.

Bria, Ion. *The Liturgy after the Liturgy: Mission and Witness from an Orthodox Perspective*. Geneva: WCC Publications, 1996.

Mahony, Cardinal Roger. *Gather Faithfully Together: Guide for Sunday Mass*, 25. Chicago: Liturgy Training Publications, 1997

Pierce, Gregory F. Augustine. *The Mass Is Never Ended: Rediscovering Our Mission to Transform the World*. Notre Dame, IN: Ave Maria Press, 2007.

9

Saying Amen

Introduction

"Amen" is a word said again and again throughout the celebration of the Eucharist. It is fitting that this final mystagogical reflection on the Mass should focus on that response of the assembly.

Background Briefing

What is the first word spoken by the assembly after the entrance procession? It usually takes people a little time to answer this question, but they get it after a little thought. It takes even more thought to name, in order of occurrence, the many times "Amen" is repeated by the assembly. It is such a simple word, said so often in response to invitations and prayers, that we tend to pay little or no attention to it. In an arresting poetic reflection on this word, Barbara Schmich writes:

> Be careful of simple words said often.
> "Amen" makes demands
> like an unrelenting schoolmaster:
> fierce attention to all that is said;
> no apathy, no preoccupation, no prejudice permitted.
>
> "Amen": We are present. We are open.
>   We hearken. We understand.
>   Here we are, we are listening to your word.

"Amen" makes demands
like a signature on a dotted line:
sober bond to all that goes before,
no hesitation, no half-heartedness, no mental
    reservation allowed.

"Amen": We support. We approve.
    We are of one mind. We promise.
    May this come to pass. So be it.

Be careful when you say "Amen." [1]

When are we most aware, most careful in saying our "Amen"? Many people will quickly identify the great amen at the conclusion of the eucharistic prayer and our "Amen" to the Body and Blood of Christ we receive at communion as such moments. We are normally very focused and conscious of saying the communion "Amen" because of the sacredness of that moment. Acclaiming the great amen three times also focuses our attention on a word said so often in the liturgy that we tend to ignore it. But it is proclaimed so much more frequently than that.

Among Christians, Jews, and Muslins "Amen" is now simply a ritual response to prayer that borders on routine. It is normally traced to Jewish (and other Semitic) roots, of which it is a transliteration. Most people know that it means "So be it" or "May this come to pass." It is also translated as "truly" in many of the sayings of Jesus. Its meaning, however, is richer than a simple ritual conclusion to a prayer, saying yes to what has been said. The root from which "Amen" comes means "to confirm, to assent, to be firm, reliable, trustworthy." Two important connotations are significant for us. One points to assenting to what is said. In the biblical context it involves believing and standing firm on what God has said. It is an act of faith, taking a firm stand on what God has said.[2] The other connotation points to being loyal and trustworthy doers of God's word. In this sense "Amen" is participative and commissive. We say not only, "Yes, it is true, we believe," but in saying that together we also commit ourselves to do our part in bringing this about. "So be it!"

What else does our liturgical "Amen" do and mean? It is a word that unites. It unites us, first of all, with one another and with the heavenly

---

[1] Barbara Schmich, "Amen," LGWO, 30.

[2] "Amen" shares a common root with the biblical word for faith. Both have overtones of not only truth but of faithfulness.

liturgy. There the angels, the elders, and the four living creatures fall on their faces before the throne and worship God, saying,

> Amen! Blessing and glory and wisdom
> and thanksgiving and honor
> and power and might
> be to our God forever and ever! Amen.

Their act of worship of the living God begins and ends with the "Amen." That "Amen" also frames and permeates our worship. It is to that heavenly liturgy that we are invited to "lift up our hearts" at the beginning of the eucharistic prayer. The great amen affirms the eucharistic prayer. It affirms our thankful remembrance of God's great deeds. It affirms the offering we have made of ourselves as a living sacrifice of praise in union with Christ and our fervent petitions for God's grace for the church and the world.

Second, the "Amen" unites us to the Risen Christ. For Christians there is in fact only one "Amen" that can be said: the "Amen" that is Christ, who is "the Amen, the faithful and true witness, the origin of God's creation" (Rev 3:14). We noted earlier in chapter 6 that liturgy is the action of the entire assembly. But also that it is more than that. It is first and foremost the action of Christ, who is the head of the Body that celebrates with him and through him (SC 7). He is the liturgist (*leitourgos*) in the sanctuary not made by human hands (Heb 8:2), where he never ceases to offer himself and preside at the heavenly liturgy. It is to that liturgy that we lift up our hearts at the beginning of eucharistic prayer, in order to join in his "Amen." Our liturgical "Amen" can be no other than that of Christ. In Holy Communion we say "Amen" to him and to his Body, making his "Amen" to God and to the world our own. Let's explore this dual "Amen" further.

"Amen" is truly a word that defines and sums up the entirety of the liturgy. A number of years ago I was browsing through the Scriptures looking for a succinct biblical way to define liturgy. I found the answer in the first chapter of Paul's Second Letter to the Corinthians. As so often happens in Paul's letters, a pastoral issue facing him leads him to a striking theological insight. The Corinthian community was complaining that Paul had not paid them a return visit, as he had promised.

> I wanted to visit you on my way to Macedonia, and to come back to you from Macedonia and have you send me on to Judea.

> Was I vacillating when I wanted to do this? Do I make my plans according to ordinary human standards, ready to say "Yes, yes" and "No, no" at the same time? (2 Cor 1:16–17)

In answer to this pastoral problem, Paul responds with this magnificent insight:

> As surely as God is faithful, our word to you has not been "Yes and No." For the Son of God, Jesus Christ, whom we proclaimed among you, Silvanus and Timothy and I, was not "Yes and No"; but in him it is always "Yes." For in him every one of God's promises is a "Yes." For this reason it is through him that we say the "Amen," to the glory of God. But it is God who establishes us with you in Christ and has anointed us, by putting his seal on us and giving us his Spirit in our hearts as a first installment. (2 Cor 1:16–22)

What caught my eye in this passage is that "Yes/Amen" is the word that sums up what liturgy is all about, saying "Amen" with Christ to the glory of God.[3] Paul's insight moves from God's fidelity and promises (always "Yes") to Jesus' "Yes" and then to our liturgical "Amen." But note that "Yes/Amen" in this passage moves in two directions, flowing out from God and then back to God. Jesus is God's "Yes" to us and to the world; he is also our "Amen" back to God. Let us unpack Paul's statement a little more, beginning with the outward movement.

First, God's attitude toward creation is faithful, it is never "Yes and No." "The LORD is faithful in all his words, and gracious in all his deeds," says the psalmist (Ps 145:13). God's fidelity to the humans is recounted again and again in Scriptures—the covenantal promise to Noah signed with a rainbow (Gen 9–17), the covenantal promise to the Israelites to guide them on the exodus and to make them a great and mighty nation (Gen 12:2; Exod 32:10; Num 14:12), the promise of a dynasty for the house of David (2 Sam 7:12–13; 1 Chr 17:11–12). That fidelity has been shown most fully in the Lord Jesus. The last words he spoke to his disciples before his ascension were this promise: "And remember. I am with you always, to the end of the age" (Matt 28:20). Paul assured his readers that the Lord's fidelity remained in effect for

---

[3] As I recall, the translation I was searching at the time rendered verse 20 something like this: "It is through him that we say the Amen when we worship."

the early Christians: "But the Lord is faithful; he will strengthen you and guard you from the evil one" (2 Thess 3:3). And even "if we are faithless, he remains faithful—for he cannot deny himself" (2 Tim 2:13). Jesus is the faithfulness of God: "For in him every one of God's promises is a 'Yes.'" In living, in dying, in rising, and in always living to make intercession for us (Heb 7:25), Jesus Christ embodies God's faithful self-giving in love, he is God's "Yes" to us and to the world. We will return to this outward movement a bit later, but first a word about the movement back to God.

"Yes/Amen" sums up what liturgy is all about. Why is that so? Our "Amen" goes through him, Paul says. Jesus lived his entire life to carry out the will of the One who sent him. That was the core of his spirituality, inherited from his ancestors; it was his passion and delight (Ps 40:8). Right up to the very end as he prayed in the garden, facing death, he sought nothing other than to do the will of God: "Father, if you are willing, remove this cup from me; yet, not my will but yours be done" (Luke 22:42). That attitude shaped all that he did and said, it shaped his entire life. The letter to the Hebrews sums up his life with these words: "See, I have come to do your will" (Heb 10:9). Jesus' entire life was an "Amen" to God, to God's will for him. We noted earlier that his life can be seen as secular worship. He is humanity's best face turned toward his Abba in full acceptance of and obedience to God's will. What other or better act of worship can we offer than joining in his "Amen"? "For this reason it is through him that we say the 'Amen,' to the glory of God." Saying that "Amen" with Jesus is possible because God has established us "in Christ and has anointed us, by putting his seal on us and giving us his Spirit in our hearts as a first installment." Jesus is the "Yes" of our ever-faithful God, and it is through Jesus that we say our "Yes/Amen" back to God. There is no other "Amen" for us to say but his. It is the Spirit implanted in our hearts who unites us to Christ and enables us to say his "Amen" as we worship God in our liturgical assembly.

We return to the outward movement of God's "Yes" in Jesus. As noted above, in living, in dying, in rising, in always living to make intercession for us, Jesus Christ embodies God's self-giving in love, he is God's "Yes" to us and to the world. If we join Jesus in saying "Amen" back to God in the liturgy, we must also join him in saying God's "Yes/Amen" outward to all people and to the world. The liturgical "Amen" is commissive, it commits us to a way of living beyond the liturgy. It must reecho in daily lives of love and self-giving service for all God's people, lives of caring for all God's creation. That is the lived "Amen" we are to say again and again in the "liturgy after the liturgy."

"Yes/Amen" beautifully sums up and seamlessly interweaves liturgy and life, saying the "Amen" and living that "Amen." Reflecting on it is a most fitting way to conclude our mystagogical walk-through of the Eucharist.

The Mystagogy

Setting the stage

Setting an environment for this session might well feature a sung "Amen." For example, invite people to sing Jester Hairston's hand-clapping version of the "Amen," a setting that originally appeared in the 1963 film *Lilies of the Field* and with which most are already familiar.[4] John Rutter's "Choral Amen" is also a fine rendition, as is the concluding "Amen" at the end of the Credo in Beethoven's *Missa Solemnis*. A poster-sized beautiful calligraphy of the word "Amen" might also be displayed with a vigil light in front of it.

Table 9A

Topic slide for PowerPoint[5]	
Title	Saying "Amen"
Visual	Amen in Hebrew [adding the following one by one:] Amen in calligraphy Amen in sign language

Attending to experience

- *What is the first word the assembly speaks after the entrance procession?*
- *At what other times in the celebration of Mass do we say it?*

---

[4] See the excellent performance by the Soweto Gospel Choir: "Soweto Gospel Choir —Amen," YouTube video, 2:45, posted by Universal Music Africa, July 9, 2013, www .youtube.com/watch?v=43dauV6tQ7w.

[5] The material in the tables is offered as a resource for facilitators who wish to use PowerPoint. The cells (rows) between darker lines in each table represent individual sample slides. The mystagogy can be conducted using only the starter questions and live interaction, if the facilitator so wishes.

Table 9B

Elicit these sequentially, in detail

- *Which is your favorite "Amen"?*
- *What does this word mean?*
- *Why do we say "Amen"?*
- *Throughout the Mass, to what do we say "Amen"*

Table 9C

Theme	liturgy = saying "Amen"
Title	Saying "Amen"
Text #1	2 Cor 1:20–22 [insert entire text with citation]
Title	Saying "Amen"
Text #2	2 Cor 1:20 [insert Scripture text with citation; remaining lines added one by one, centered, as in text below]
Text #3	Rev 3:14 [inserted at bottom of slide with citation]
Title	Saying "Amen"
Text #4	2 Cor 1:21 [insert Scripture text with citation; remaining lines added one by one, centered, as in text below]
Title	Saying "Amen"
Text #5	"Amen" [read the poem and at the end insert the last line:] "Be careful when you say 'Amen'."

Recap

Table 9D

Themes	Amen with Christ to God—worship Amen with Christ to world—mission Amen sums up both liturgy and liturgy of life
Title	Saying "Amen"
Visuals	Amen image overlay: Hebrew, calligraphy, sign language added one by one as in the topic slide

Texts

#1—2 Cor 1:20–22

"For in him every one of God's promises is a 'Yes.' For this reason it is through him that we say the 'Amen,' to the glory of God. But it is God who establishes us with you in Christ and has anointed us, by putting his seal on us and giving us his Spirit in our hearts as a first installment."

> (2 Cor 1:20–22)

#2—2 Cor 1:20

"For in him every one of God's promises is a 'Yes'." (2 Cor 1:20)

> in living
> in dying
> in rising
> in always making intercession
> Jesus Christ is God's self-giving in love
> God's "Yes" to us & to the world

#3—Rev 3:14

"The Amen, the true and faithful witness, the beginning of God's creation."

> (Rev 3:14)

#4—2 Cor 1:21

"For this reason it is through him that we say the 'Amen,' to the glory of God." (2 Cor 1:21)

> Christ's "Yes" to God is our "Yes" to God
> his "Yes" to others & the world
> must become our "Yes"

#5—"Amen," by Barbara Schmich (LGWO, 30)

Be careful of simple words said often.

"Amen" makes demands
like an unrelenting schoolmaster:
fierce attention to all that is said;
no apathy, no preoccupation, no prejudice permitted.

"Amen": We are present. We are open.
We hearken. We understand.
Here we are, we are listening to your word.

"Amen" makes demands
like a signature on a dotted line:
sober bond to all that goes before,
no hesitation, no half-heartedness, no mental
reservation allowed.

"Amen": We support. We approve.
We are of one mind. We promise.
May this come to pass. So be it.

Be careful when you say "Amen."
(Barbara Schmich)

Reflective Resources

Bernstein, Eleanor, ed. *Liturgical Gestures Words Objects.* Notre Dame, IN: Notre Dame Center for Pastoral Liturgy, 1995.

Ramshaw, Gail. *Words around the Table*, 120–122. Chicago: Liturgy Training Publications, 1991.